UP THE SMOKE

Shoddy Town Tales

Fred Butler

illustrated by Graham Kaye

FAB Publications Mirfield West Yorkshire WF14 0PU

First published in 2001
by FAB Publications
Eastfield House
Flash Lane
Mirfield
WestYorkshire
WF14 0PU
Tel/Fax 01924 49249

© 2001 Fred Butler
This edition © 2006

Produced and distributed
by Jeremy Mills Publishing Ltd
www.jeremymillspublishing.co.uk

ISBN 978-0-9540683-0-1

Illustrations by Graham Kaye
Brighouse West Yorkshire 01484 712752

Cover illustration
"Bradford Road from Crackenedge"
Bruce Mulcahy

I bent my student back yet again as I stooped wearily to pick up two more of the frozen lumps which masqueraded as bricks. It was a clear spring day on Rawfolds in Cleckheaton but the overnight frost had bitten hard, and its teeth-marks lingered on in the frozen building materials all around me. The bare skin of my fingers stuck to the icy blocks as I loaded them into my heavy black wheelbarrow, each pair of bricks ripping its freeze-welded layer of flesh from my soft academic palms.

"Why am I subjecting myself to this tortuous anguish?" I ask my inner academic self. Returning from my comfortable London existence only two days ago in early April 1964, why didn't I take time to live the life of Riley for a day or two, idling the lazy hours away in the Yew Tree or in the bookies' down our road?

Looking back, I'm glad that I didn't.

Instead, I went out of my way to do as many different jobs as possible while it didn't matter so much. What I didn't realise then was that work was an important part of my education in "learning about Life" as they say.....

And where better than in the Shoddy Towns of Dewsbury and Batley!

Dedicated to

My long-suffering family

who have all put up patiently with my
nostalgic ramblings for many years

and to

David Moss

who left the field long before the final
whistle

CONTENTS

Introduction

***

UP THE  SNICKET

Stand beneath the railway arch at the junction of Bradford Road and Halifax Road. Watch the persistent winking of a multitude of traffic lights and look up. High above you, plastered in a black and white banner on the side of the once-austere mill, read it with pride:

EST 1856

MACHELL BRO^S LIMITED SHODDY & MUNGO MANUF^{RS}

It shouts the news to all who pass in their railwayed comfort, a clarion call from yester-year. A lingering testament to the Shoddy Towns, it demands your attention: "Oh, thee! Passenger on yon train! Tha'r in Dewsbury, nar, sithee". If you hadn't realised it, you're at the very heart of the Heavy Woollen District. True, the mill is now a block of flats, dominating the station arches in all its splendour of nineteenth century stone. And yes, the bottom floor has become "Kiddies Kingdom", but as you risk a crick in the neck staring up at those words on high, at least it tells you something of whence we came.

Ever since Frank and Dennis Parr got their eighteenth century heads together to create padding for posh folks' chairs and called it "shoddy", the inhabitants of Dewsbury and Batley have regarded themselves at the arse-end of society. We were second raters, weren't we? *Our* daily task was to snatch back some brass from muck-ridden cast-off rags, clawed out from the bottom of humanity's pile of detritus, and to make it fit for gentle-folk to park their nethers. A century and a half of such activity has produced an inferiority complex as evident as Quasimodo's hump on each Shoddy Town shoulder. "Look at us!"

i

we yell to all who stare. "We're from Dewsbury - tha can't tell us nowt." Labouring under the strain of our grammatically incorrect war-cry, we make our brash way up the narrow ginnel between Tithe Barn Street and Westgate and in through the narrow doorway of the Little Saddle. Time for a pint or two...

But what if you're *not* a native of the Shoddy Towns? What if your Dad dragged you here from the depths of rural *Cider-with-Rosie* country when you were only eleven? What if the big, brash Batley lads at the Grammar School button-hole you on your first play-time up against a playground wall - a country bumpkin, from whom they can extract the human water? And what if Form Bully's friendly hand fastens menacingly round your throat with the hissed instruction to "say summat" for the general entertainment and delight of the assembled crowd of leering jackals?

Well, you join them, don't you? At the beginning of that long-ago summer of 1957, Yorkshire was a far-away land of Norse Gods, Flat Caps, Mill Chimneys and Puddings. But come the autumn, after my transplant to the North, my gentle West country tones are soon ridiculed out of me. In less time than it takes to smoke a genuine Woodbine, I become one of the lads as I play naughty tricks in the street on Mischief Night, get up to no good up the snicket at the bottom of Carlinghow Hill, and learn the staggering truth about a Washbowl Willey. I am a Shoddy Town lad through and through, and *no* bugger takes the human water out of *me*....

Down the cobbled streets of the last forty years, I've wandered the dirty, dusty length of Bradford Road, in and out of those long-gone dark, satanic mills. In their gloomy

ii

shadows, I've met Dopey Don, Cuckoo and Eric the Fireman; I've joined the KOYLI's and watched Horsfall shoot a sheep; I've caused bother at the Palace in Heckmondwike and I've been to *the* Palace to shake HRH by His Royal Hand. I've supped Hammonds Bitter in the ale-houses of Batley and Dewsbury whilst earning, learning and laughing with genuine Shoddy Town folk, so I reckon I've earned my spurs as a Yorkshire lad. My tales are really *their* tales - taken from the rich tapestry of life at a time when the cobbled streets of Dewsbury and Batley were still cobbled, Taylor's mill-chimney still belched thick black smoke and the "Shoddy Towns" featured in Geography text-books the world over.

Fred Butler

January 2001

SHACK

BAKER! Those socks! Go home immediately - and don't come back!"

The Beak's booming tones echoed across the quadrangle of Marling Grammar School on a bright West Country autumn morning in 1956. We first year boys shivered in trembling anguish on our way to morning assembly as the black-gowned Vampire's gaze tracked icily along his file of young charges. Eyes averted reverentially, we contemplated our own hose down to the hem of our regulation long short-trousers, our gaze stopping at the ends of our bare 11 year old legs. But there was little to worry about. Baker was a Fifth Former and had been spotted by Dr Annett, our revered Headmaster, wearing lime green fluorescent socks which shouted defiantly from the bottom of his grey school flannels.

With a meek and hang-dog slump of his shoulders, the adolescent offender made his way out of the quadrangle muttering a submissive "Yes, sir" and we never saw him again - ever. Expelled *sine die*.

So this was life at my new school, was it?

After the euphoria of passing the 11+ exam and the prize of a new bike - Palm Beach Tourer with straight handlebars and dynohub lighting - I was soon swallowed up into the culture of the place. I accepted unquestioningly the social procedures of life in a boys' grammar school of the Fifties.

There were boarders - boys who actually slept at school - and there were Prefects who had an oak-pannelled Common Room off the Main Hall where we "fags" were obliged to make their toast for them at break times.

There was a bespectacled Music teacher called Watson whose son was in my class. In our first-ever lesson on crotchets and quavers, Watson [father] cheerfully knocked Watson [son] over the back of an old wooden school-desk as a hefty ear-clouting example to us all of his classroom discipline. This guaranteed my lack of interest in music for the rest of my life, along with a similar apathy towards numbers [except for those with a sporting connection*]. This phenomenon was spawned by a young Brylcreemed Mathematics teacher called King. On long summer afternoons, when all our adolescent stirrings were longing for the great outdoors, he droned and mumbled in his sincere efforts to educate us numerically. But he only succeeded in boring the school-grey pants off us.

And, of course, in the West Country, there was that abomination of a game which calls itself Rugby Union....

But, despite all that, it is hardly music to my ears when my Dad announces that he is about to make a career move and that we are to up sticks and move North - to Cleckheaton at the heart of the Heavy Woollen District of Yorkshire. In my youngster's misinterpretation of things, I picture coughing old fogeys bent double under the great weight of their cardigans. They all wear flat caps as they wend their way past dark satanic mills to be swallowed up in the cavernous gloom of ancient weaving sheds. I spend a fortnight or so in tears.

However, I resign myself to my fate and we left Stroud and the Cotswolds that summer. I began to contemplate the prospect of starting over again at a grammar school in Batley where, above all else, they played *proper* football [Association]. At this prospect, I was reasonably pleased until I attended on my first day and I was shown into a classroom already occupied by twenty-five or so Batley lads. Standing at the front of Screwy Lewie's Chemistry class, I fell under their rugged, threatening scrutiny. None of them, it appeared, had ever come across a country bumpkin with a Gloucestershire accent before and they took great delight in reminding me of the fact.

* For example:	Notts County 6	Arsenal 0
Or	1. Arkle	8-1
	2. Desert Orchid	100-30
	3. Red Rum	6-4 fav

"Say summat," was Form Bully's instruction at my first break-time, up the snicket on the top cinder track, a huge meaty fist held menacingly a few inches from my face.

"Oi don't know what Oi orter say," was my reply, which prompted gales of laughter from the assembled cronies and which resulted in an overnight change of daily speech such that I was taken for a native of the Heavy Woollen District within about a week of my arrival.

"Put wood in t'oil," I would say with the best of them. I learned to chant a rhyme which began: "We're all darn in t'cellar-oil wi' t'muck-slakes on t'winders........" and I used to ask regularly: "What dusta think tha'r on - thi father's yacht???"

📖 Lesson Number 1: Learn to adjust rapidly to your changing circumstances.

By the time I had progressed to the Fifth Form, I had become accepted as a sporting, womanising smoker who was not frightened of Saturday morning detention for failing to wear his school-cap on the way down Carling-how Hill to the bus-stop and home. I had joined the K.O.Y.L.I. school detachment of the Army Cadets but I wasn't averse to taking a Friday afternoon off school to accompany my great pal Norreth to his house for coffee and Woodbines. I knew how to wait for girls [from the Girls' Grammar School] in the Bus Station without causing a fuss to the local folk and, most important of all, I knew how to sup a pint in the "Black Tulip" or the "Anchor" down Dewsbury on a Saturday night.

📖 Lesson Number 2: Learn the art of behaving badly. It beats well-behaved conformity and it's much more fun.

But the school lesson which has stuck with me most poignantly for the remainder of my Shoddy Town life concerns "Shack". Richard Shackleton - a round-faced, round-bodied youth, smaller than the rest of us, with an unbroken adolescent whine of a voice; a hanger-on in the Bus Station and the butt of many cruel remarks about his roly-poly appearance and his Pear's Soap Bubbles hair. "Podgy" or "Big Dick" had to take it all on the chin with a wan smile, as we "lads" heaped derision upon him on a

3

daily basis. And he continued to smile obsequiously at all our humorous remarks while Form Bully encouraged us to perform a variety of foul tricks on him for the general amusement of the whole form.

📖 **Lesson Number 3: Join in with the bullying - then they won't turn on you**

A mouthful of spit, secretly gobbed on to the end of a comb, could be flicked with a fair degree of accuracy when the master's back was to the class, to land on Shack's open exercise book. Any noise of protest from the victim would earn a "Saturday" from the irate master or a playground head-butt [in Shoddy Town Speak, "stickin' t'neb on"] from Form Bully. So he learned to keep his complaints to himself. On his tour of the silently bent backs of 5Alpha, the master would seize on Shack's besmirched book, the ink still wet and smeared with spit, to deliver a board-rubber blow to the back of his head and to issue him with a "Saturday". How dare he be in possession of an unsatisfactory exercise-book!

You could also have enormous fun with an ordinary pin from your mother's sewing box.

In the days of boys changing into pumps for indoor wear [to protect the corridors and floors?], it was a simple job to ram the pin, from inside the pump, through the welt at the toe. This was your weapon, for secret use in class...

A careful wait until the master's back was turned, and a well-aimed kick from the sitting position would deliver the stabbing blow right up the bum of the boy in front, whose nethers would hang over the rear exposed edge of the ancient oak and iron school-desk. Form Bully always managed to find a desk immediately behind Shack's fat adolescent arse and would await the appropriate silence of classroom endeavour before deftly delivering the fatal blow. The sudden release of an anguished cry was inevitable, as was the master's retribution, so Shack would end up with further board-rubber bruising and another "Saturday".

📖 **Lesson Number 4: Learn to laugh at the pain and misfortune of Shack [and thank Heaven that it wasn't you]**

4

Then came _the_ moment to remember for the next 40 years.

It was a winter's day in 5Alpha's dinner-time form room where Fifth Form boys were allowed to proceed with their academic studies instead of being ejected for an hour and a half into the winter chill of the playground along with all the other kids. The weather was foul, the room was warm and Form Bully was at the height of his bullying career...

Shack had already been poked, squeezed, insulted and berated by most of us and there was a dire need for a fresh diversion to while away the dinner-time study period. It came by way of the roller-board, standing idly in the corner, the remnants of the morning French lesson still clinging dustily to its fabric face.

Form Bully discovered its main feature: it was double-sided, hinged at the centre and could thus be swung over to reveal a clean reverse - all black, shiny and ready for - banging on Shack's head. After some of us had pinned him into the corner preventing his escape, this was great entertainment indeed - a rhythmic thumping on Shack's pate along with witty remarks like "You're singing like a lark, Richard - a pillark!!!"

📖 Lesson Number 5:   Always laugh at Form Bully's witty remarks - for safety's sake

During the five or ten minutes of the rhythmic bashing, it occurred to Roy to rifle through Shack's school-bag.

"Ey up, Big Dick - is this your bag?" he enquired in a falsely obsequious tone.

"Course it is, yer twat" [Richard was becoming annoyed.]

Perceiving such anger in an instant, Roy turned to the window, lifted it open and emptied the entire contents of Shack's bag onto the playground, two floors below. Pens, books, shorts, cig. packet and a miscellany of school-boy articles cascaded to the ground, and with their rapid descent, Shack's temper burst. Much to our amusement, he ranted and raved and cursed and swore, and with a

5

superhuman effort, overturned the roller-board, scattering boys [including Form Bully] to the four corners of the room as we dived for cover.

Through gasps of tearful anger we caught the words "I've f...ing 'ad enough now, an' I'm OFF!" Crashing through desks and overturning chairs, he stormed out of the room, pursued by hoots of derision and gales of raucous laughter. This was top-drawer fun but, after rejoicing, discussing and recounting the incident, it wasn't long before we lost interest and the room sank back into normality.

Homework books were consulted, pens sucked and chewed in earnest thought, Log Tables thumbed through, and the incident was long forgotten.

📖 **Lesson Number 6:** Learn to over-ride your conscience - forgetting your wrong-doing is easy.

Later that afternoon, we were summoned from a History lesson to Headmaster F.W.Scott's study - five or six of us, snivelling and white with fear - we knew that this was Trouble.

Francis Willoughby was a fearsome ex-army officer with an Oxford degree, a head of shiny black hair and eyes which pierced your very soul. He specialised in frightening us Batley lads with his odd-ball Army behaviour which was far beyond our social understanding. And you weren't summoned to his inner sanctum unless there was some dire business afoot.

Had one of us failed to turn up for Saturday morning detention? Which one of us had been caught smoking? Who's been hanging about in the Bus Station, annoying the lasses from the Girls' Grammar School? We examined our collective consciences on the way down the corridor towards the office, near the front entrance to the school. But the reason for our summons should have been obvious: Shack had run off home and told his Mum, and she had telephoned the Headmaster and now it was our turn to be bullied - in the arse with the Boss's cane - or so we thought...

We stood shame-faced, eyes cast down to stare at his Head-master's carpet, a thick silence filling the room. He glared at us, seethingly quiet, his black eyes flashing anger.

An eternity passed and the afternoon sunlight made his hair and gowned figure appear even more satanic than usual. Without saying a word, he turned to a time-worn oak cupboard behind his desk, slid back the door and produced a rolled up poster. Unravelling it with a flourish, he revealed a starving Biafran child, thin and emaciated, eyes gazing imploringly at the camera. Craning forward at us and with a Shakespearian edge to his voice, he hissed dramatically: "*This* .... *is Shackleton!*"

To us Batley lads of 1961, his words meant little. We had to stifle and choke our uncomprehending and embarrassed laughter until the journey home across the Mud Bath, when we mimicked and mocked our Headmaster's efforts to touch our collective consciences.

"I nearly wet mesen," chortled Form Bully. "This is Shackleton!".

"What were 'e on abaht?" I asked in plaintiff style [note the accent], playing to the crowd but knowing all the while the answer to my stupid question. By now, I'd begun to feel the pangs of guilt. What we'd done to Shack over the past six months was unforgivable and cruel in the extreme, but it couldn't be undone. "What wor that picture o' that kid all abaht?"

"Buggered if I know" said Norreth

"We gorra Sat'dy aht'n it, any rooad," whined Roy. "That means wes'll 'ave ter miss football for t'school."

Forty years have passed and I now believe that I am qualified enough at the University of Life to understand what F.W. Scott was getting at. But his ploy failed miserably as the incident passed into the history and folk-lore of BGS, 5Alpha, 1960-61. Failed, that is, until quite recently...

Having kept in reasonably regular touch over the inter-

7

vening years, my good pal Norreth rang me about two months ago.

"Hey, have you heard about Shack - he'd just come back from Egypt - he was a Civil Servant or something - and he'd gone shopping down Batley, and he dropped dead outside Woollies. Heart attack. T'funeral's on Wednesday."

📖 **Lesson Number 7:** **If only the clock would run backwards...**

***

IF  ONLY ...

"Come on! Come on! Open the bloody shop before mi soddin' bus comes..."

I hopped up and down in exasperated anguish outside the Bar House - the corner shop near the bottom of our road. Mrs Mitton shuffled towards the front door in her slippers, a large brass key in her hand, ready to commence the unlocking process. She shot a darting, piercing glare through the glass. "We don't open till 'alf past, yer know, an' it's nobbut twenty past..." was her genteel, customer-service welcome.

"Yer, Ah know, Mrs Mitton, burr Ah'm aht o' cigs..."

By this time, the big red number 20 Yorkshire Woollen District Transport omnibus [Leeds-Mirfield via Batley] would be pulling up at the Yew Tree, one stop before mine. A crowd of brown-blazered Heckmondwike Grammar School kids would be clambering on board, and I'm still conducting my first commercial transaction of the day.

"Five Woodbines, please, Mrs Mitton," I smarmed and down on the counter clanked nine large, round, Britannia-backed coppers. In return, Mrs M. presented the small, slim, light green and orangey-brown packet of "Wild Woodbine" cigarettes. Those magic words were angle-bannered in blue across the ornately designed background and the letters:

"W.D.& H.O. WILLS BRISTOL & LONDON"

filled the orangey-brown strip across the bottom. A joy to behold and just the right size for concealing behind the neatly ranged text-books in the dark recesses of my school-desk.

I grabbed my hard-earned treasure gleefully and hurtled out of the door as the Number 20 squeaked to a rumbling halt outside. Breathless, I boarded the open platform at the rear and made my way upstairs into the warm hubbub of Heckmondwike Grammar School kids, took a rear seat and settled down for the three mile journey to Batley, relishing the prospect of a nice, relaxing smoke...

If only I'd listened to that long-haired tramp in Amsterdam that time when I was fifteen and we were on a school trip! But you   know how it is when you're young. A stupid, scruffy old git in a mucky raincoat wasn't going to tell us anything. We were from Batley Grammar School, weren't we? And we knew absolutely *everything* there was to know about absolutely *everything*.

Now, a few years before this overseas experience, at the age when most kids of my generation were learning to swim, I did just about the daftest thing I've ever done in my whole life. It was all down to those Blacklock brothers and a bloody telephone box - the old red sort with small panes of glass on all sides and a big black safe-like case inside. Emblazoned on the front of the safe, in big white letters, was the sign "Button 'A'". On the right-hand side, out of sight, was "Button 'B'" and the Blacklock Boys had invented a financial enterprise which revolved around the latterly mentioned Button B. Such an activity was capable of raising a whole shilling in pennies, without any one having to so much as break into a sweat, and, in view of the fact that Kenny was Top Man in our gang [and our Independent Financial Adviser], we went along with any scheme he invented. Besides, it sounded like Heaven-on-Earth to me - ready cash and no hard graft involved...

But looking at it through this end of the telescope of time, I wish someone had taken me on one side on that bright summer's afternoon, just before Kenny Blacklock had come up with his brilliant idea, and given me a right good preventative kick in the nethers ...

Like most kids during the long afternoons of the six week holiday, we were hanging about on the corner of Welland Close with very little to do. Red-haired and multi-freckled Tom Macalpine suggested football in the short-grass field, but it was too hot for that. Thin, angular Coggie, dressed like the rest of us in his long short-trousers, proposed a game of Monopoly on his back lawn, but it was too hot for that. Short, fair-haired Mickey Morgan felt like going up to the level-crossing to put tanners on the railway-line for the 2.45 to Kings Cross to flatten them into shillings, but it was even too hot for that.

Eventually, as you've probably guessed, it was one of those Blacklock boys who came up with the ultimate proposal.

"What we need is some nylons," announced Kenny, the leader of our gang from the "prefabs" just behind the school. "An' then yer stuff 'em up t'Button B 'ole an' leave 'em for a week. Who's off ter swipe some, then?" and he cast his piercing, accusing look over us gang-members. When K did that, and you're only nine and he's eleven, you succumb to the social pressure, believe you me!

"An' wes'll need a bit o' strong wire ....Our Ronnie, you can get that when we need it," continued K. "Then we're off to t'telephone box near t'park - nob'dy'll know us round there. An' after a few days, wes'll be rich!"

Now, although not a lot of what Kenny was saying made much sense to us at the time, we went along with it because it was Kenny, and what he said went. Anyway, if you chickened out now, you'd be shown up in front of your mates, and none of us was having any of that, thank you very much.

So it was, a couple of sunny afternoons later in August, 1953, our gang of six or seven kids made its way from this end of town along the leafy streets to Wilton Park at the other end, where nobody'd know us. A quick, secretive rifle through the wash-bin had failed to provide me with one of my Mum's nylons. In fear of Kenny's subsequent castigation if I'd turned up with nothing, I furtively grabbed a huge pair of bloomers which I proudly produced when we drew near the big red telephone box, ready to make our fortunes.

I managed a wan smile as K. passed the stolen article

round for all to inspect. "Is thi' mother in t' Air Force, then? Is this 'er parachute, eh?" Huge guffaws all round, as the rest of them heaved a sigh of relief that our Leader's scorn wasn't being heaped upon them, and then down to the serious business of the day...

From a respectable distance, we watched an old lady shuffle across the street in her slippers and enter the box, all prepared to make her call.

In those days, before you got through, you first of all put your three large shiny coppers into the slot on the top of the big safe-like box and listened to them clank down into the machinery. Then you dialled your number with your index finger on the silver wheel staring at you from the front of the large black telephone. If you got the cheery "Hello" from the other end of the line, you pushed in a large chrome Button 'A' on the front of the big black box, your money shuttered down and you had your three penn'orth of chat. But if you didn't get an answer after a sensible wait, then you pressed Button 'B' on the side of the box and down the shiny chute at the bottom rolled your three shiny coppers, saying: "Try again later, pal."

So now, following Kenny's instructions to the letter, we waited on the corner under a spreading laburnum tree, looking for all the world as if we were about to go and play in the park. "*Don't* look at that bloody telephone-box....pretend we're waiting for t'ice-cream van ... Look over t'wall and whistle..."

And eventually, the coast is clear. Quick as a flash, we race to the telephone-box, K. in first, out with the the left leg of the bloomers and shoves it up the Button 'B' chute, out of sight.

"Wire," he hisses to Ronnie with a snap of the fingers, and he rams those bloomers up the chute as far and as tight as he can, so as no would-be caller will ever spy them. And all this time, the rest of us are keeping a careful look-out to make sure nobody spots what he's up to.

"Reight," says Ken. "That's it - we're off" and, somewhat

baffled, I join the sprint across the road and into the park, eventually to flop breathless onto the grassy bank beside the lake...

"Is that it, then," I said, feeling a bit let down. After all, we hadn't done anything more exciting than mess about in a phone-box. Some of the other younger ones in the gang were seemingly just as baffled.

"Yeh," whinged Coggie. "'Ow can yer get rich from doin' what we've just done?"

K. pronounced wisely and mysteriously on the subject: "Now we 'ave ter wait - while next week, 'appen - an' when we come back, wes'll be rich!!"

The day after, from the estate opposite, along comes Old Codger complete with walking-stick, waistcoat, muffler and flat cap, to make a call to their Alice in Leeds. His three shiny pennies are at the ready as he enters the box and follows the correct procedure.

But their Alice isn't in, and after about two minutes, he presses Button 'B' for his money back. He hears the rattle of his pence, but nothing appears down the chute. He bashes the box a few times with his stick, even broddles about up the chute with his boney, arthritic fingers, but K. has done an excellent ramming job and there is absolutely no way those three coppers are going to worm their way past my Mum's compressed underwear. So Old Codger leaves the box cursing and swearing and complaining about modern inventions. Threepence out of a pension... That would have bought fish and chips and a bus ride into Dewsbury when he was a lad... And nowadays, it was the price of a phone call...

Well, to cut a long story short, a few days later, Kenny and the rest of us arrive on the scene. Using the wire again, but this time bent into a hook, Ronnie Blacklock broddles it about up the Button 'B' chute and gives it a twist. From outside the box, we hear the musical clatter of a week's worth of shiny coppers tumbling down the chute as Ronnie yanks out the left leg of my Mum's old drawers. K. pockets the brass and we make off into the

13

wide blue yonder, five pairs of young legs in long short-trousers whirring like bees' wings, as we high-tail it, Hopalong Cassidy-style, back to our side of town to count our winnings.

"One and nine!" gasped Tom Macalpine in wonderment. "One and bloody ninepence - we can go to t'flicks on that!"

"Who can, yer daft bugger" scorned Ronnie B. "It costs a tanner in - so there's only enough for three on us and threepence change."

Kenny, a true Socialist at heart, cuts short the speculation. "Wes'll 'ave ter spend it on summat for us all," he announces imperiously, "An' I know what.......Follow me," and he points in the direction of Luxton's shop.

Ten minutes later, and we're all at the shop on the corner of Union Road deciding who should go in and ask for ten Woodbines and a box of matches. And so, at the age of nine years of tender youth, I came into contact with tobacco.

In those days, nobody really bothered about its effects on either lungs or wallets. It didn't matter where you were - on the streets, at home, in the Saturday afternoon "Rex" or "Essoldo" staring intently at the big silver screen - just about everybody dangled a "cig" between their fingers and spoke their words whilst exhaling great clouds of blue, de-nicotinised tobacco smoke. So it's no surprise that we lads fell for it without so much as a moment's thought about what we were letting ourselves in for.

So there we were, ready to do the business and K. is laying down the law again: "You'll be t'best Freddie, 'cos you're t'tallest, an' if 'e sez owt, tell 'im they're for yer father." So up the steps crept yours truly, not wanting to be shown up in front of the gang and, at the same time, frightened out of my britches because I knew I was doing something wrong.

"That'll be one and six and tuppence for t'matches, Freddie. Burr Ah thowt yer dad allus smoked Player's. 'As 'e swapped over to t'cheap 'uns then, and lost 'is lighter?"

14

"Eh..oh...yes, Mr Luxton. 'E says 'e likes 'em better....and 'is lighter's run out o' petrol." And in the twinkling of an eye, I was back out on the pavement clutching a green and gold packet of Wild Woodbines and a box of "England's Glory" matches.

"Quick, let's scarper," shouted Ronnie Blacklock. "Down to t' 'oller tree."

The hollow tree last mentioned was exactly that - a long dead tree that time had hollowed out, standing in a little wooded copse, surrounded by fields out by the railway line leading off to Leeds and Scarborough and other such exotic places. Generations of nine and ten year old lads had spent time in there, using it as a sort of Den Headquarters where the long days of childhood activities could be sorted out, planned and organised.

It was vitally important that nobody saw what we were up to or, for that matter, how we'd come by the money, so we all six of us entered the hollow tree at the bottom and arranged ourselves in ascending order right up to the top. Look-out was Ronnie, his head sticking out of the top of the trunk about fifteen feet above, just like one of those soldiers in an armoured-car comic-strip from "The Rover", "The Hotspur" or "The Adventure".

The Woodies were shared out ["every cigarette bearing the signature *W.D. & H.O. Wills*"], the matches passed up the tower of lads, and the magic moment arrived at last!

In the musty, damp dark of the tree-trunk, about 12 inches below Coggie's left trouser leg, everything I'd laboured for - pinching my mother's knickers and the long week of waiting - was captured in this snap-shot of childhood. Strike the match, light up and suck in a mouthful of sweet Wild Woodbine smoke...

And it was *foul*! What did anybody see in it? Sucking smoke in and blowing it out again, leaving a rank bad after-taste; flecks of vile, bitter tobacco sticking on your tongue making you spit? But not one of us was going to admit to such unpleasanteries and risk isolation from the gang. Oh no! We stuck to our guns like little heroes, sucking and pulling on our Woodies right down to the tab-end, enveloped in clouds of billowing blue fumes which rose from the smoke-stack of the hollow tree.

If any doubts about the pleasures of tobacco were on the point of surfacing, Big K. came to our rescue.

"Nar, yer don't smoke like that. To do it reight, yer've to do t'swaller." And he showed us how.

Already a seasoned smoker, Kenny helped himself to one of the spare Woodies and proceeded to demonstrate the art of inhaling. At the time, I can remember standing in gob-smacked awe, eyes popping, as Kenny leant nonchalantly up against the hollow tree, talking _and exhaling smoke at the same time, just like John Wayne or Robert Mitchum!

By now, feeling brave, we'd all ventured out into the open, puffing our Woodies for all to see, knowing that there was nobody around for miles.

"First off, yer've to gerra gobful o' smoke an' then y'ave ter tek a deep breath - so as ter gerrit reight dahn inter thi lungs," boasted Ken. And lo and behold he did it once again for the benefit of his appreciative and admiring audience, blowing out clouds of blue smoke into our faces to emphasise the point.

"Reight - Ah'm off ter do it nar..." I said and proceeded to mimic Kenny's action. A long pull, puckered-up mouth, clenched   teeth, and then draw breath like a Titanic survivor coming up for air. The others gazed admiringly as starry lights appeared on my personal horizon,my temples throbbed and a horrible sick feeling welled up in the depths of my stomach. I landed flat on my back in the long grass, feeling decidedly ill - with a disgusting churning sensation in my stomach and a roaring buzz in my ears. I dragged myself onto all fours, head down like a naughty dog.

"Ey up, Freddie, are y'awreight", asked Ronnie, expressing genuine concern. "Tha's gone green."

"Yer - Ahs'll be reight," I replied manfully, seconds before fetching up the entire contents of my stomach into the lush green grass at the back of the hollow tree...

After that, I left smoking well alone until I got to the Grammar school and fell in with the members of the "bacca party" - the lads who went down the banking at the far end of the school playing field every break-time for a fag. Well, I wasn't going to be left out, was I? Quite soon after, at the age of twelve or so, I was "doin' t'swaller" with the best of them, thus necessitating setting off five minutes early to catch the bus for school each morning.

With a cheery "So long" to my Mum, I would sprint desperately down to the Bar House shop, fervently hoping that Mrs Mitton had opened up early. If she had decided to to stay in bed for a bit longer, I would have to opt for the threepenny bargain, available at Mad Jack's shop near the bottom of Field Hill - one Woodbine and two matches. "Threepence, please - for your smoking pleasure" .

All of which brings me back to that old tramp...

It's 1960 and we're big men now - Fifth Formers - with free time on our school trip to Amsterdam. We're out on the town, drinking beer and smoking duty-free cigs till they're coming out of our ears. Norreth, Jack Hirst, Tate and myself had settled ourselves down on the verandah of some Dutch bar to take the night air and to do some serious drinking, when a scruffy, unshaven tramp with long, flowing, fair hair engaged us in a one-way conversation from the pavement.

"You'll regret that you know," he said in perfect English, pointing accusingly at our cigarettes. "You want to stop now, while you've still got a chance...." and he proceeded to capture our interest by telling us all about how he'd been in the desert during the war at the battle of El Alemein, chasing and killing Jerries. Him and Montgomery had been moving so fast that their unit had advanced way beyond the supply lines, so the squaddies couldn't have their rations of rum and round tins of Player's Navy Cut cigarettes.

17

"Ey up, Freddie, are y'awreight? Tha's gone green."

"...and do you know what, boys, I had to stick my head in a bucket of water to stop myself wanting one of those," and he pointed dramatically at my cig. "Because it's a drug, you know," he announced, like a vicar at morning service. "*Nicotine is a drug!*"

Did we listen to him? Was he a tramp in a mucky coat spinning us a tale? Were we too pissed to care? There's no proper answer to any of these questions. But if only I'd listened to him and taken it in, I'd have saved myself a hell of a lot of wallet trouble...

The other day, having nothing better to do, and just out of idle curiosity, I sat down at our kitchen table and worked out how much I've spent on cigarettes since 1956. Take an average cost of £0.85 per day, to allow for the fact that you don't buy as many when you first start out on the daft habit. And then - Oops, wait a minute, they've just gone up again in the last Budget to £4.27 for twenty Woodies - so make that £0.92 per day... and then work out the number of days in forty-six years [forget Leap Years] and multiply them together and that'll give you your final total of ...... **£16,111.00!!!**

If only I'd listened!

I might as well have got all of the sixteen grand in nice, new, crisp tenners, taken them out onto our back lawn and set fire to them - because in effect, over the past forty-six years, that's exactly what I *have* done!

***

19

THE UNFORTUNATES

Have you noticed how there's always some poor sod who seems to catch all the stick that's being dished out, no matter what? You can see him coming towards you, along corridor or crowded street, and something about his appearance immediately unlocks the computer filing-system in your brain. It might be his looks, his bodily parts or his clothes, but whatever it is, the law of the jungle, as instilled from an early age at your all-boys secondary school, dictates that you must get in first. So you listen carefully to any scathing remarks which might be passed by your "mates", thank the Good Lord above that they haven't turned on you, and deftly file the object of their derision neatly into the appropriate folder. And there you are - he's stored away for future reference. Next time you want to appear good or when someone looks like having a go at you, or even when you're short of something to talk about, all you have to do is flick open the folder and shoot out the barbed comments.

However, if you're feeling *particularly* vulnerable or unsure of your ground, the next time you see the poor sod in question, you nudge your mate alongside, give him a wink and open up that file, ready to use any witty remarks and Smart Alec sayings that might come to mind. You shout them out for all to hear, without a moment's thought for the hapless butt of your remarks. I call such people "The Unfortunates", because everyone knows who they are only minutes after first clapping eyes on them, and from that point on, they're always going to be on the receiving end of life's kicks, thumps, jibes and clever remarks.

Now as time has progressed, I reckon I've got the Unfortunates classified into six different folders, and each one is good for hours of cheap fun and belly laughs galore...

📂 FOLDER NUMBER 1   SPOTTIES

Around about the age of thirteen, some kids develop an entirely new outer coating. A sort of volcanic eruption explodes all over their faces and their entire complexions are made up of red and yellow craters.You can't miss these craters - they glow in the daylight a bit like the flashing beacon on top of a breakdown truck, so you can see a Spotty coming at you from *miles* away. But of course, the Spotty is doing his best not to be noticed, so he shuffles along looking ever floor-wards, thus developing a permanent Richard the Third/Quasimodo hunchback. Not only that, he's trained his hair into a sort of permanent balaclava helmet, so as to cover his face. But that won't do him any good at all, because as soon as you spy him on the horizon, you access the "Spotties" folder, nudge your mate and make ready for sharp remarks.

"Ey up, Zitty! Ain't it time you had a wash - you're changing colour!"

The best one I heard was my old school-mate Tate who, upon spying a Spotty on the top corridor one break-time, performed a very credible imitation of Little Richard's '50's hit "Babyface" but changed the first line to: *"Craterface, You've got the cutest little craterface..."* He sang it all the way down the stairs to our classroom, long after the Spotty in question had disappeared into the toilets to hide away. I chortled gleefully as I filed that one - straight into my "Spotties" folder for future reference, ready for the next one I came across, or the next time I came under fire.

📂 FOLDER NUMBER 2   SPECKIES

Ever since the invention of the damned things, spectacles have given generations of school-kids a ready supply of sarcastic verbal ammunition. Look around you and there's always bound to be some poor sod who has to wear sight-enhancers in order to perform even the simple tasks in life. So he goes straight into the folder for clever remarks.

But more often than not, it's the type of glasses that a

Specky wears that determines the amount of stick he receives. Some glasses seem to be worn unnoticed, causing the wearer no hassle at all, but others shout at you from the Specky's face, just asking for comment.

When I was a lad, it was those National Health spectacles which caused all the fun. They were very basic articles of seeing apparatus - just bits of wire wrapped round bottle-bottom glass lenses - but they had the ability to make certain wearers resemble a wide-eyed goldfish swimming round a bowl on the window-ledge of life.

During the long summer-evening games of football on the "rec", a Specky always ended up being "selected" to play in goal where his glasses wouldn't get knocked off and broken. He would therefore spend the entire evening swimming backwards and forwards between the goalpost coats, only involved now and again when desperate defenders failed to prevent opposition forwards from bearing down on the Specky goalkeeper.

Inevitably, this *always* happened at a vital moment in the keenly fought contest, and the Specky concerned *always* let in a vital goal. At such times, everybody opened up their Speckies folders and came out with remarks like:

"Bloody 'ell Specky - I could 'ave stopped that wi' mi' willie - get yer eyes chalked and clean up thi' gigs*..."

Or: "Well, yer four-eyed git - tha wants ter get thi glasses fixed afore tha goes totally blind....." Or: "Yer blind bugger - tha owt ter chuck them gigs o' thine in t'bin - or tek 'em back an' ask for thi brass back..."

Of course, Speckies couldn't win. Even if they pulled off a magnificent Lev Yashin** save at a crucial time in the game, we would stand back in amazement and make gob-smacked utterances like: "'Ow could 'e 'ave seen that through them bottle-bottoms???" Or "'E only stopped that 'cos 'e thowt it wor a mucky mark on 'is gigs."

* gigs: Shoddy Town slang for spectacles

** Lev Yashin: Top-drawer USSR World Cup goalkeeper of the '60's

And so we come to the most unpleasant "Unfortunates" folder - the one which is full of Life's Stinkers.

Sometimes, through no fault of their own, some people just *smell*, don't they? This may be due to a general lack of personal hygiene, to repeated dribbles of pittle down the knicker-leg or even [on the Thursday following] to a week-end curry. In any case, as grown-ups, we're all rather tolerant in our treatment of such people, but when you're young and at school, it's often a completely different matter...

The one I always remember from my junior school days is Stinker Merritt.

We never knew him by any other name. From his matted, unwashed mop of lank, black hair right down to the raggy hem of his '50's long-short pants, he gave every sign of being neglected at home. But worse than that, he just *stank*. A combination of stale wee, bad breath and unwashed body gave him a permanent four-foot ring-fence of foul stink wherever he went. *Everbody* avoided him. None of us wanted to spend play-times with him; he was never selected in any playground football/cricket games; and - most important of all - nobody wanted to sit next to him in class.

Poor old Stinker - at the front of our village-school classroom, he occupied a double desk - one of those old-fashioned jobs with a cast-iron frame and a hinged seat - all on his own, banged up against the big iron stove which was the heating for the whole high-roofed, high beamed Victorian classroom. He was isolated in a cocoon of his own pungent aroma, shunned by both Teacher and pupils alike the whole summer long.

But come the Jack Frost season...

That old iron stove was the sort you see in the Sherrif's office in Lone Ranger cowboy films or in soldiers' billet rooms in 50's war films, and it had to be early morning coke-stoked-and-lit by Mr Trickett, the School Janitor. We used to dread the winter months when the ice lay thick on the playground and the bare flesh on your short-trousered legs turned a blotchy play-time purple-orange. We didn't fear the numbing aches of limbs and digits thawing out as waves of heat from the ancient apparatus beckoned you in for the next school-room session; and we didn't give a jot for the fact that our feet were soaked and blue from trailing about in the snow. No, what struck terror into our young hearts was the prospect of searing waves of mobile warmth from the fully-functioning stove which would pass by, over and alongside Stinker's desk. On their way past him, they absorbed his stench, and convection currents of stiflingly stale-wee stink would swirl in great clouds round the January school room, bringing tears to everyone's eyes.

As if that wasn't enough, and to add to this hazard, Teacher's desk was always right next to the stove, up-wind of Stinker's place. Immediately in front of it, strategically placed, was the last classroom place on earth where *any* of us wanted to be at *any* time during the school year - within stick-swiping distance of Sir. Any minor out-of-season transgression anywhere in the classroom was punished with a move to the front desk and a period of time "under the cosh". At least you were some safe distance from Stinker, so every cloud had a silver lining - but not in Winter.

Now, Teacher had another string to his disciplinary bow, and the nasty swine would often use it as a punishment:

"Ah! Freddie Butler - is that you talking again? Well you can sit here, in front of my desk where I can keep an eye on you [dramatic pause for effect] ..... "*next to Merritt!*"

Many a time, after a particularly vigorous and sweaty session of play-time football, the crafty ones amongst us would quit the game immediately the bell went and hare off into class. If you tried to pinch a bit more playing time after the bell, and you were last in the line filing into class, the horror would mount at the slow realisation of your fate as you plodded dutifully onwards. By the time you reached the threshold of the room, your so-called mates - Mickey Morgan, Donald Beard, Mervyn Scrivens and the rest - were all grinning knowingly at you from the safety of their seats at the back, while your eyes became fixed on *it* - beckoning you like a Siren onto the rocks - the last and only seat available to you in your entire classroom world - next to Stinker!

With liberal use of the handkerchief over the air-intake orifices, you make it through the next hour or so, and dash gleefully into the playground to take in great gulps of clean, unsullied Cotswold air.

📁 FOLDER NUMBER 4   FATTIES

This "Roly-Poly" folder of kids is an extremely fertile source of adolescent fun. Fatties are a bit like Spotties in that they can't hide. They are always on display, so it's easy to get at them. At the black-board jungle of our Grammar School in the late '50's, taunts and jibes about "blubber" and "podge" were all accepted as part of the fun-experience of growing up, but life must have been very unpleasant for the Fatties. Walking about in a body which trailed and splodged folds of fat everywhere, they earned nick-names which stuck. What nick-name is more evocative of a wandering lump of young, blubbery, lethargic lard than "*Plosh*"? It ought to be recognised as a verb in the Oxford English Dictionary:

> **plosh:** [vt]   to move slowly and deliberately from one activity to another; to labour arduously in the effort to move excess body weight;to flollop around like a whale in search of water [Origin obscure; probably HWD slang circa 1950]

Nowhere was the discomfort of a Fatty greater than in the showers. After games sessions, when the rest of us readily stripped off and frolicked under the steaming warm jets, making jokes about each other's willies, the Fatties would perform an endless variety of delaying tactics to avoid joining us: knotted boot-laces, lost soap, lost towel, urge to pee necessitating 20 minutes in the toilet; urge to check yesterday's Maths homework. But it was no use - sooner or later, they would fall under the hawkish glare of "Basher" Smith - Loughborough-trained and a strict disciplinarian.

"Come along, sonny - shower..." and the Unfortunate

25

would "plosh" his way towards the steam-shrouded noisy banter at the far end of the changing-room. Once he was in there, the fun became physical as well as verbal. Form Bully would inevitably dominate proceedings:

"Look at 'im, trailing fat everywhere - it's rollin' off 'im - are yer sure y'aven't left any outside...?

"'Ave we ter see 'ow far we can gerrus fingers inter 'is fat...?" and with this remark, he would make menacingly for the poor Fatty, wielding a stubby adolescent forefinger, while a couple of cronies barred the way out. As Fatty cowered up against the tiled wall, the finger would be rammed into the rolls of belly-fat and clever remarks would follow:

"'Ey up! It's gone reight in up to mi elbow - Ah think Ah've lost mi arm - Ahs'll 'ave ter gerrin an' 'ave a look." And the jape would finish with a mock attempt at climbing into the folds of fat, finishing with a knee in the genitals which brought tears to the eyes of poor Fatty.

📂 **FOLDER NUMBER 5**   **SNOTTIES**

These chaps were renowned for the two strips of glistening green, slug-like slime which permanently trailed down the upper lip from the nose, never quite reaching the mouth. For some inexplicable reason, we used to call these slime-trails "candles" when we were young, but there was no resemblance to the paraffin-wax affairs we could buy at the local shop when there was a power-cut. Snotties deserved the derision they got, because they always looked dirty and wore holey cardigans and, more often than not, they were always without a handkerchief to wipe away the offending articles. Sometimes, the cheeky buggers would ask to borrow yours! This encouraged lying:

"Sorry, pal, it's in the wash." or "'Aven't got one 'cos mi Dad's borrowed it for 'is work."

But this is the magicians folder! Snotties were masters of the disappearing trick. Glance at them across the classroom or in the crowded playground and see the "candles" gleaming brightly in the morning sunshine, freshly dribbling down the upper lip. Look away for just a second and you're likely to miss it. The candles have gone - vanished without trace; sniffed back, vigorously defying gravity, into the darkness of the nasal passages, to stay snug and warm until their next excursion into the open air. Ten minutes later, there they are again, poised dramatically, $^{1}/_{16}$ inch above the lip.

Left too long in the fresh air, however, and candles would turn a darker shade of green as they became encrusted, thus rendering them removable only by a back-swipe of the cardigan arm across the top lip. Once again a vanishing trick *par excellence* but this time, evidenced by a woolly-jumper cuff hardening to a yellowish-green cardboard as the weeks rolled by!

🗀 FOLDER NUMBER 6   ODDBALLS

The final folder is best called a "spare". It is full of Life's Unfortunates who don't happen to fit into any of the other easily recognisable groups but who nevertheless come in for a fair amount of stick. They stand out for a variety of reasons: long hair, funny walk, cross-eyes, strange genitals, odd speech - to name but a few. Often they can be easily identified by a nickname which helps to place them into the Oddballs folder without giving the matter too much thought. Fancy walking through life, remembered by your school mates as "The Methley Monster", "Ronnie Ringpiece", "Flitsy Titsy Fleapants" or simply "Pigfart". A moment's imaginative thought on your part, however, and you will come up with a host of answers to the question: "What do they call 'em that for?"

All these "Unfortunates" shuffle their arduous ways through life, their individual journeys made more difficult by our sniping and nasty remarks. They soldier on regardless, often smiling and joining in with our so-called "fun" to divert the flack, to avoid any trouble or to save face. Their internal despair, deep down in the depths, is truly desperate - if only they might escape for a while and become "normal" like the rest of us, life would be so much more fun. But years after we tossed them aside and moved on to the other, more serious pastimes of life,

27

they're still there, grown up now, proper living people leading normal lives, having found their fun at last.

Each and every one of them deserves our greatest respect for their courage in getting through it all. One of them - from Folder Number 6 - has mine. Without *him*, I wouldn't have gone to the Palace and met HRH and had a conversation with the great man - but that's another Shoddy Town tale ...

***

RASTUS

Don't ask me how he came by the nickname of Rastus, because I just don't know. He was a Birstall lad whose proper name was Copsey - and he was in the "A" form, so that made him one of the school's elite. Amongst us lads, however, he was an Unfortunate - quiet, withdrawn, long-haired and deep-voiced. Rastus shuffled along corridors and around classrooms, cocooned in his own academic world, eyes permanently fixed on the floor. The live-wires in his form made his life miserable by pushing him around and calling out his nickname with an exaggerated 650 Norton revving sound, so it came out as "Rrrrrrrrrrrrrrastus".

In the darkest depths of a Mathematics lesson, be-gowned Charlie Spurr would rasp threateningly across a silent classroom: "Who spoke ???", wielding the threat of a Saturday morning detention like a scimitar in battle.

The "braver" members of the class would sometimes suggest : "Sir, it wor Copsey...." This was their vain attempt to earn the angelic Rastus a sinful black mark in Heaven, but it rarely worked.

Rastus was never in trouble for the simple reason that he hardly ever spoke directly to anyone - most of his remarks were addressed diffidently towards the floor. When he was asked a question in class, his deep, educated mumble would echo across the room with the right answer, prompting break-time sarcastic imitations: "Mumble, mumble, Pie-R-squared, sir, mumble... "

As you might expect, when the character-building oppor-tunity arrived to join the school CCF*, one of the first hands up to be counted was that of sensible, mature Rastus. But of course, the Army section was not for him. Oh no! He joined the Brylcreem Boys in the RAF section - the swots with brains from the "A" form.

Not for him the stripping of the .303 rifle and the Bren

* CCF   Combined Cadet Force

gun or the treks round school with a field radio chanting meaningless military mumbo-jumbo "Papa Lima; Papa Lima; Papa Lima. Calibrate on this frequency. I'm off down t'banking for a sly swaller*. Over..."

No, Rastus learned about flying and wind-speeds and went up in a glider - *intelligent* stuff for the *intelligent* lads of the "A" form.On Duke of Edinburgh's Award activities, however, we were all thrown in together and that's just about where this tale begins...

I'm looking at my little green record book now as it sits on the desk in front of me. It resembles a half-size passport, official-looking and sombre, with the royal crest still shining out in gold as does the lettering:

THE DUKE OF EDINBURGH'S AWARD
RECORD BOOK

Inside, the first page has been completed in my own adolescent hand: *Date issued: December 1959.*

On page five, the printed text is distinctly 1950's in tone:

This scheme is applicable to boys after their 14th birthday and up to their 19th birthday.

There are three series of tests, each of which represents a different level of achievement, applicable as follows:

The First Series - from the age of 14 upwards.

The Second Series - from the age of 15 upwards.

The Third Series - from the age of 16 upwards

Then there are pages of tests to be completed and further on, there are spaces to be filled in and signed by assessors when you've passed. Most of the tests were tailor-made for the competitive atmosphere of Batley Grammar School in the '50's.

Of course, the powers-that-be at the school were *very* interested in those boys who could reach *GOLD* standard. If you got stuck on Bronze level because you couldn't chuck a cricket ball more than 180 feet, then chuff your

* sly swaller   illicit intake of nicotine [See "If Only..."]

luck, pal - you were a Has-been and a Failure - down amongst the dead men.

Now, if there was one of these tests which was designed to tax your adolescent initiative to the full, it was Section B: *The Expedition*. Dreamed up by one of HRH's boffins, it was a typical activity of its time - all chaps together under canvas ["minimum three, maximum six"]. Assist each other to traipse across open/wild countryside, carrying all your chattels - food, clothing supplies *and* your mobile home [A-pole, three-man tent] - on your back! From camp to camp, you were a team, each member working for the good of all the others in an effort to pass that test and gain that award...

I well remember my first training Expedition, starting at Keighley Station one summer Friday evening in the company of Fawcett, Charlesworth, Ramsay, and Laing [last two named from RAF section and the 'A' form. Me, Ken and Charlie, berks from Army Section and the 'Alpha' form].

We were commanded by Corporal Burgess - big, beefy and amiable, a born leader of men; and Aircraftsman Wilde - big, beefy and crazy, not averse to biting sizeable chunks from anyone who offended his oft-perverted sense of justice. Both were in the Upper Sixth and they were responsible for general discipline and training as we arrived at our first camp-site for the night. This was a small field belonging to some farmer who was very pleased to welcome BGS lads to his back yard in the Dales.

The spirit of team-work prevailed as Army Section Berks attempted to erect A-frame tent in the gathering gloom. RAF Brylcreem Boys had theirs up in seconds and began cooking evening meal, wafting tempting and delicious smells of steak fritters across the evening air.

During this time, far from assisting their trainees in the practice of tent-erection, our leaders Burgess and Wilde had discovered a rare and absorbing pastime. Having come across a small working horse tethered in a little low-

31

roofed barn for the night, they proceeded to excite it by chucking lighted matches into the darkness and chortling at the nag's obvious distress as it tried to kick its terror-stricken way out of the dark prison cell.

After about an hour's-worth of such fun, midnight struck on some distant Dales village clock and we three Alpha-form lads eventually inserted our hungry, adolescent bodies into our sleeping-bag cocoons. We contorted our bodies round boulders and projections under the ground-sheet of our amateurishly erected tent, and settled down for a night of well-earned, blissful slumber...

The next morning, I awoke to find my arms lovingly clasped around Charlie's middle, while Ken Fawcett had spent the nighthalf under the Dales starlit sky, his bare arse sticking out from the flysheet to welcome in the dawn. But that was but a trifling concern compared to the arrangements for breakfast...

Still sleep-logged, we rummaged round in our rucksacks and eventually came across some "Dried egg". According to our carefully prepared expedition plan, this was to be our first meal of the day so we set to with a will. Charlie, Ken and I struggled manfully to light our primus-stove; we struggled manfully to fetch our water; and we struggled manfully to make the yellow powder resemble anything like egg.

But RAF chaps Ramsay and Laing had got this expedition lark off to a fine art. While one of them deftly and expertly lit the primus and assembled the lightweight, collapsible frying pan, the other produced several thick rashers of bacon from the depths of his rucksack. It wasn't long before the delicious aroma wafted on the crystal early-morning air up the slope towards our tent.

We looked at the pathetic, pale mixture spilling like pewk off the sides of our plates onto the green earth, and would gladly have committed murder for a rasher or two of that crisp, aromatic pig-meat. But no such offer was forth-coming. Instead, those Brylcreem Boys sat smugly relish-ing each last little morsel, even dipping their bread in the fat to emphasise the point, while Charlie did his best with a billy-can full of water and we had to be content with scalding our lips on a tin-mugful of brown, brackish tea...

By now, you'll be asking the question: "But where does Rastus fit in?" Well, the answer lies in the Cheviot Hills! That's where we were despatched to complete our expedition for the Gold Award, some three years after that first training attempt from Keighley station. "A 4-day journey covering at least 50 miles in wild country"- that's what it says in my little green record book.

Well, the country was wild, the weather was bleak and the only thing you could hear for miles around was the pathetic bleating of several nice-looking Scottish Lowland sheep. There were seven of us altogether, including Brylcreem Boy Rastus, as we arrived at the very border between England and Scotland on the A68 at Carter Bar. All kitted up with our mobile homes and our supplies on our backs, we waved a cheery goodbye to our smiling teachers who had supervised us this far, and set off up the steep slope at the road-side into the uninviting wilderness of Knox Knowe...

On the second day, following an uncomfortable night's sleep on boulders stuck between the shoulder blades, and in the uncharacteristically blistering heat of the afternoon, we marched cheerfully on our Gold Award way and longingly anticipated arriving at the next camp-site and a welcome spell of Rest and Repose. However, as we passed close by Spadeadam and a top-secret rocket range, a growing sense of doubt began to wash over the entire group.

After about an hour's march, frantic perusal of the map and liberal use of the compass indicated that we were lost! Fading in spirit somewhat, we dragged our heels through thickening gorse and squelchy peat-bogs until, quite out of the blue, we came to a stoney roadway.

This was an unexpected delight. Since such a route *must* lead to *somewhere,* a slight spring returned to our steps as we continued on our way, still unable to locate our precise position on the map.

Pondering the existence of several red flags erected on high poles in this barren, God-forsaken area, we trecked along the dusty roadway, heads down and rather dejected. Were we going to fail this final test, the coveted Gold Award slipping uncontrollably from our collective grasp, as we became more and more lost?

The contemplative silence of our private sorrow was shattered by the roar of a jeep round the next bend and the sudden realisation that we were surrounded by some half-a-dozen proper soldiers - *with guns*. Five of them crouched down beside the track, casting watchful glances at the surrounding hills while their Leader, who had obviously modelled his military bearing on Desperate Dan, strutted up to us. Sticking out a huge, black, stubbled chin, he enquired in caring military fashion, after our well-being:

"What the f...... hell do you think you're playin' at?" he roared, his finger hovering frighteningly close to the trigger of the sub-machine gun which was resting in the crook of his severely tattooed forearm. "Can't you read? This is Army property. Can't you see those f...... flags?" and he waved his free hand in the direction of the distant purple hills.

We were about to provide answers to this searching interrogation, but were cut short by a succinct command which demanded no response whatsoever: "F... off back where you came from," he growled, menacingly.

We readily complied, turning tail and running, which is extremely difficult when you are encumbered by the mobile home on your back, but fear proved to be a great motivator. As we became mere specks on the horizon, the military men leapt into their jeep and disappeared in a cloud of dust - Mission Accomplished. The throb of their engine faded away into the oblivion of the Cumbrian moorland, and we slowed to a canter to take stock of our position...

34

All that time spent taking compass bearings and orientating the map to the land, which had been such an important part of our CCF training back at school, had turned out to be as much practical use as a chocolate teapot!

We were completely lost and the panic mounted as we scanned the far horizon in a desperate attempt to spot some identifying feature which we could locate on Ordance Survey Sheet 86. But wherever you looked, there was nothing except rolling, heather-covered hills, wide-open blue skies and the far-off bleating of a blasted sheep!

There were no tall mountains, village churches or railway cuttings with which to establish our position. As a result, we'd wandered round and round, traipsing the Borders countryside for hours on end, in grave danger of disappearing up the bum of the man in front! Our carefully planned route to take us from one camp-site to the next had vanished into thin air and with it, our hopes of clearing this particular hurdle on our way to passing the Gold Award series of tests. Complete and abject failure was staring us between the eyes and it showed in our haggard, care-worn Shoddy Town faces ...

There was nothing for it but to sit down for a few hours, admit failure and await rescue by the Assessors, who would no doubt miss us at the next check-point and alert the emergency services. An air of utter despondency and gloom settled over us all - particularly the A-form Brylcreem Boys - how could *THEY* of all people consider *FAILURE*? One of them actually began to blubber as he realised how close we were to a total cock-up. What would we tell them back at school? What would our CCF Officers and our Mums and Dads have to say? It was all too awful to contemplate.

As the truth gradually dawned on us and we realised that we weren't going to receive our Gold Awards, you can just about guess what happened next. Instead of the occasional bleats of sheep, the air was filled with the griping sounds of Batley lads blaming each other for their current predicament:

"Yer useless pillock - tha couldn't read a map if thi life wor on it...."

"We're bloody lost nar, an' it's all down to thee - allus walkin' off in front, yer lanky bastard..."

"An' in the next cage, ladies an gentlemen, we have the Fookahwee Tribe, known by their characteristic tribal war-cry: "Where the Fookahwee??"

"Stop pissin' about now - what we bahna do?? Wes'll never gerr 'ome now."

But while everybody was cursing and blaming everyone else, and the Cheviots air rang ever more blue to the sounds of our Shoddy Town rantings and ravings, Rastus it was who quietly and deliberately picked up the discarded Ordnance Survey map, sat on a bit of jutting rock and took out his "Silva" compass.

After about five minutes of careful calculation and much studying of the sky-line, he announced diffidently to the heather-covered floor, in true Unfortunates' style: "I think I know where we are."

Well, of course, nobody took any notice at first because we'd spent six or seven years ignoring his quiet remarks, and we carried on arguing and shouting until someone said, "Tha what, Rastus? What did ta say?"

"That grassy knoll in the distance is where we should have been had we followed compass bearing 187 degrees," he droned in his deep rumbling Unfortunates' voice, not used to having people listen to him."In fact," he mumbled, "we have become disorientated by our failure to correctly calculate the mean difference between Magnetic and True North and as a result we have strayed off course in this valley at Slighty Crag..."

He pointed knowingly at the map. "I think if we were to follow compass bearing 96 degrees along this ridge, we ought to regain our correct route."

We gaped incredulously. In our entire BGS lives, not one of us had ever heard Rastus put more than two or three mumbled words together. But *now* we listened with the undivided attention of toddlers at Mummy's knee, clutching at the ever-strengthening straw which was Rastus's growing confidence. For the first time in his scholastic life, he surveyed his captive audience, eye to eye, as he indicated a purple-topped ridge in the far distance with a dramatic sweep of his forearm.

So now, we followed Rastus's instructions unquestioningly and to the letter because, probably for the first time in his school career, *he* was in charge. He led the group from the front, waving his arms and pointing, stopping every now and then to check the map. We followed on behind like obedient cocker spaniels on walkies in the park, knowingly nodding our agreement at his observations. And to cut a long expedition-story short, he was absolutely spot-on!

After masterfully rejoining the correct route, Rastus led us to the next appointed camp-site where we thankfully bedded down for the night, exhausted by the extra miles of unplanned walking. We slept the sleep of utter exhaustion which comes from a heady mixture of relief and gratitude to the most insignificant of our number - Rastus Copsey.

In my Record Book, under the heading "The Expedition", amongst other remarks, the assessor has written:

CHEVIOTS   23-26 April 1962

*He took his due share in the planning and
preparation of the expedition, which was carried
out as planned, the party showing good team
spirit, even when delayed by minor mishaps..."*

What a hoot! "Minor mishaps" meant we didn't have the slightest clue as to where we were! Our "team spirit" was down to Rastus the Unfortunate and his superior navigational powers. Without them, we'd all have failed the test.

None of us would have walked up the steps of the Portrait Room at Buckingham Palace with our Mums and Dads in tow, all spruced up in our Sunday Best and looking as proud as Punch. Not a single one of us would have had his picture in the Batley News alongside a report with the banner headline: "*West Riding youths at the Palace*". None of us would have shaken hands with the Duke of Edinburgh himself or, in my case, had a conversation with HRH about the town of Batley and how hard I'd worked to get the Award.

At nineteen years of tender youth, this awkward, gangling Shoddy Town youth had a word or two with Prince Phil! My Mum left the Palace on Cloud Nine, already drafting a detailed and graphic account for the Townswomen's Guild and all the neighbours back home!!

So at last I've come clean about my achievement all those years ago. And I sincerely hope all those A-form Brylcreem Boys have remembered the events on the Cheviot slopes in 1962 as they left the Palace and pinned on their Gold Award lapel badges for the rest of their lives.

We owed our success to a long-haired odd-ball who shuffled through his school career looking down at the floor, the butt of sarcasm and cruel remarks.

The real leader of the team was Rrrrrrrrrastus. What a hero!

***

K.O.Y.L.I.

You know how it is. You're fourteen and some *very* Important Person comes along and asks your group or class whether or not you'd like to join *this* Organisation or *that* Society. Well, you just look away in your adolescent embarrassment, don't you, hoping that Important Person won't pick on you and say something like: "...and what about you, young man? *You* look as if you'd enjoy basket-weaving as a hobby. Aren't you going to put your name down?"

Well, you can do without any of that, thanks *very* much...

Throughout April and May 1959, amongst the "Lads-That-Mattered" in 3Alpha at Batley Grammar School, talk was dominated by the subject of volunteering to become a member of the Combined Cadet Force. "Joining up" meant surrendering a great deal of your free time to the King's Own Yorkshire Light Infantry CCF, but it was generally viewed by the Grammar School Establishment as a fine, character-building experience for the young chaps from the back streets of Batley.

All volunteers began their CCF careers as Army recruits, but if you were *really* clever, you might progress to the RAF section - even learn to fly! Such an elitist organisation suited the 1950's Grammar School system down to the ground. It was based on earnest endeavour and striving to be first, best and top dog. Everybody was in with a chance of promotion if they played their smarmy cards right.

But *not* in 3Alpha!

For weeks, Form Bully had made it clear to all of us in the form that anyone volunteering to join up was a soft prat, "daft in t'ead" *and* a swot. Such a person deserved the scornful contempt of the entire school. He promised total banishment from The Lads-that-Mattered crew, plus unceasing sarcasm and piss-taking as a result.

Throughout the form, we nodded vigorously in agreement as Form Bully issued his thoughts, so our collective decision was as solid as a rock - not open to negotiation of any kind.

When the moment came, it was a matter of honour: "Keep yer marth shut and yer 'and dahn."

So, for 1959 at any rate, projected recruitment to the BGS KOYLI division of the CCF was going to be very poor indeed, judging by break and lunch-time conversations:

"Ar' ta bahna join t'cadets, then?"

"Me??? Catch me dressin' up to laik at soldiers on t'front yard? Not bloody likely!"

Or:

"What dusta think abaht joinin' t'cadets, then?"

"Tha bloody what? Fartin' abaht wi' all that drill an' marchin' an' campin' at week-ends? Tha must be off thi chump if tha thinks Ahm 'avin owt ter do wi' it. *Not in a month o' Sundays, pal!*"

So it was decided then, and the moment duly arrived.

Captain D.N.R. Lester - actually Head of French but also Officer Commanding the School Detachment of the CCF - did his annual tour of the Third Year classrooms one hot, July afternoon. He was on his annual quest to obtain a commitment from us to join up for the next two years [four years if you were going into the Sixth Form]. Of course, in 3 Alpha, the outcome was going to be in no doubt whatsoever...

Striding into the classroom, DNRL addressed us from the front in his austere tones: "Now, listen to me," he drawled. "I have a very important question to ask you. Are you listening? Good..." He cleared his educated throat with an imperious cough. "Listen, then. The question is this: Who is going to join the CCF?"

I pictured the scene behind my front desk as I looked away from D.N.R's piercing gaze.

All eyes would be averted to the floor and hands would be

shooting into pockets. *"Keep yer marth shut and yer 'and dahn."* Nobody was going to show themselves up by volunteering to join in, and a thick silence began to fill the room...

I stared in anguish at the floor in front of my desk, dreading the moment that I might be singled out.

"Ah, Butler, I'm sure you'd enjoy using a field radio, wouldn't you...?

But the agony of that moment never materialised. Instead, I heard D.N.R.L's educated tones making a list: "Yes, good. Who have we ... Pearsall, Charlesworth, yes... ah... Fawcett, Good. Sawdon... Yes, jolly good."

I looked round in amazement. All those "knockers" who weren't going to join the Cadets as long as they had holes in their arses had shot their hands into the air the moment the question had been put, leaving us gullible berks way behind in the race to volunteer.

To his eternal credit, Form Bully kept his hand firmly in his pocket and, sticking to his proverbial guns, he glowered round the form, leaving me to my conscience and better judgement in the decision whether or not to take the Queen's shilling.

D.N.R.L. spun smartly on his heel to leave and shot a parting remark at us over his shoulder:

"Very good, 3Alpha...Very good. Fourteen of you. Now listen carefully... Are you listening... Another very important question... Anyone else before I go? Last chance..."

The blood rushed to my head and pounded in my ears; the sweat rose on my brow; my face flushed crimson as I thought to myself "Oh stuff Form Bully" and I let out with a daringly diffident "Yes please, sir. I'd like to join."

I glanced across at Form Bully. Behind his big meaty adolescent hand, he mouthed the word "Wazzock" and our relationship cooled for a while during the subsequent week or two. But that first rush of blood soon slowed to a trickle when I began to ruminate over my hasty decision.

41

The entirety of my spotty youth, it seemed, was about to be dominated by dressing up as a khaki clown on Friday afternoons and floundering about on the front yard for the entertainment of those kids in the lower-floor classrooms who dared to sneak a look.

Was there a way out, I asked myself in quiet moments at home. Could I produce a pacifist's note from my Mum to excuse me? Might I develop a mystery illness which prevented me from marching for any length of time? Should I run away from home? Try as I might, I could not arrive at a satisfactory solution to the problem and in the end, I resigned myself to my miserable military fate...

So, on the first Friday of the Autumn Term, 1959, I dressed up in my ill-fitting khaki uniform, strapped my well-blancoed gaiters round my ankles, grabbed my school-bag and prepared to serve Queen and country for the next four years.

The cynics from Heckmondwike Grammar School had a field-day taking the rise out of me on the bus until they alighted at their school, and they left me crimson with rage and adolescent embarrassment to continue my journey.

All the way over Healey and on to the stop at the bottom of Carlinghow Hill, I seethed, until I stepped down onto Bradford Road and suddenly felt much more at ease. The street was full of awkward and gangling adolescents all very similarly attired.

We were all sporting uniforms which were ten sizes too big for us; we all clomped up the hill to school in our regulation issue black leather marching boots; we all wore green berets which ballooned out sideways at right-angles above our right ears, defying the wind and gravity.

I met Charlie half-way up. "Ey, but this khaki's rough on thi' skin, innit, " he moaned. "Mi willie's bin rubbed raw sin' Ah left 'ome - Ah berrit drops off at break-time..."

"Tha'r not wrong, Charlie.... It feels as if someone's attackin' mi bollocks wi' sand-paper."

42

We moaned our way throughout the day's classes, regularly checking our important bits for wear and tear, until 3.15pm. And then, along came the first of the perks of joining up.

While the rest of the school yawned its way through lessons until the welcome week-end bell, we KOYLI's assembled on the front yard for a parade - released into the fresh air forty-five minutes earlier than the others. We paid no heed at all to the fact that the rest of the school would be scooting homewards at 4.00pm whilst we "soldiered" on until 4.45pm. Early release from the boredom of Maths or French was music to our ears.

Besides which, once on the front yard, we came under the beady, watchful eye of Sergeant Pell...

Smart, stocky and squat, Sergeant Pell was a Man of the World. He swore vividly; his fingers were stained a golden brown from heavy smoking and he told tales of drinking and womanising in faraway places.

Precisely and immaculately turned out in the uniform of the day, he was a Squaddie who had seen the seamier side of life. A regular soldier from the nearby Pontefract Barracks, his job for the first hour of CCF time was to knock our drill skills into shape - and to us Batley lads, he was a Hero.

He treated us as raw recruits, struck the fear of Army discipline into us and earned our undying respect. We listened with fearful joy as he cursed us into shape, his sharp army voice slicing through the Friday afternoon peace, rudely awakening the classroom-bound "civilian" dullards from their French lessons. To us, "Pellmanism" was a fiery brand of military discipline, not a mind-training method for exam revision.

"'Ow do we drill in time, eh? eh? We count, don't we. [*quietly and menacingly*] You can all count, can't yer - yer should be able to - you're all at the bloody *Grammar* School, aren't yer? Watch and I shall de-monster-ate the Right Turn....

[*Shouts in falsetto*] Squad! [*Squad jumps with fright*].

43

Pearsall wets himself. Sgt Pell returns to normal square-bashing tone] Squad will move to the right in three's.... RIGHT.... [*pause, during which we think he's buggered off home for his tea*] .... TURN!!! [*Sgt Pell turns smartly to the right, whilst counting the movements*] ONE, two-three; ONE, two-three; ONE two-three; ONE! [*This last ONE! delivered in high falsetto*].

Needless to say, it took us quite a while to master the art of Pellmanism or "Drill", as it was better known. Why is it that there's always some poor sod who cannot come to terms with the art of marching? Such a person insists on throwing both arms forward as soon as he is instructed "By the left, Quick ... MARCH" and he makes his stumbling way round the drill square [front yard], lolloping along like a rag-doll with rickets. This often annoyed Sgt Pell.

"SQUAD....Halt! PEARSALL! You are marching like a c..., laddie! Ave you got summat stuck up your arse? On the command "Quick March", what do we do, eh? eh? Right arm forward, left foot forward, left arm back. Like so: Quick....March! [*delivered in falsetto*] ONE!"

Such simple instructions confuse "Perse" for about three weeks as he tries in vain to distinguish his left arm from his right foot, but he, along with the rest of us, eventually masters the physical nuances of the activity. So, after four weeks of regular front-yard Pellmanism, we knit into a fairly well-disciplined squad, able to handle the complexities of drill with or without .303 rifles.

A few weeks later, Sergeant Pell is in top mischievous form.

"I will now de-monster-ate that any drill order on the drill-square has a Command clause and an Executive clause. So as soon as you hear the first bit, you know what's coming next, and you carry it out, don't you, eh? eh?. For instance: [*returns to parade-ground decibels*] Squad will move to the left in threes.... LEFT..... [*returns to normal voice-register*] ..... And you know what's coming next, don't you lads??? [*sarcastically*] 'Cos you're all clever buggers what goes to the *Grammar* school! Yes, it's "TURN". But we knew that already, didn't we lads? Eh? Eh?"

We nod, dumbly, not altogether following his military drift.

"Let me show yer. *[Parade ground decibels again]* SQUAD! *[We become alert but hold the "at ease" stance]* Squad will move to the right in threes RIGHT ..... *[We guess - intelligently, 'cos we're all clever buggers from the Grammar School - what drill order we are about to be given]* ..... SHIT!

[As a man, we execute a perfect King's Own Yorkshire Light Infantry Right Turn] "ONE, two-three; ONE two-three; ONE two-three; ONE."

With a knowing and amused gleam in his eye, Sergeant Pell turns crisply on his heel, lights up a Senior Service and marches smartly off the front-yard parade-ground into the military mists of time...

*

If drill with Sergeant Pell was a necessary but not too unpleasant evil, then firing .22 and .303 rifles was a positive joy.

You see, my generation of fourteen year olds had been weaned and brought up on vividly told real-life tales of El Alemein, D-Day, Arnhem and the annihilation of Adolf's Third Reich.   Practically every story-book, comic or ABC Saturday morning film featured True Life stories from the War, so the killing of vast hordes of Jerries with a .303 rifle or a Bren gun was as natural to us as using Log Tables to solve quadratic equations! But to actually fire those weapons in open countryside using live ammunition was like re-living the past - a real treat of Christmas Present proportions! So with great relish, we boarded the hired coach on "Range" days and travelled to Hawksworth, on the moors above Baildon, for a day's shooting.

But oh, how that eager, youthful relish and anticipation

rapidly dissolved into anguish! Oh yes, our comic-book heroes shot Jerries by the cart-load, firing their .303 rifles classically from the shoulder, but nobody mentioned to we young readers that the minute you squeeze the trigger, the bloody weapon kicks you like an angry ten-ton mule with toothache ...

So for the first time ever, I sprawled my scrawny six-foot frame on the firing point, took aim at the distant target and squeezed the trigger. As the live round crashed smartly up the barrel, hotly pursued by burning gases, I was certain that my ear-drums had burst and I *knew* that my head had been blown off. But that was nothing at all compared to the mighty clout the recoil delivered to my thin, meatless adolescent shoulder.

The long pointer from the butts below the target indicated a "wipe-out" [complete miss], the bullet zipping off into outer space as I failed miserably to control the business-end of my gun.

Thereafter, I devised various methods to protect my puny body against the onslaught of the .303's recoil. One of my most successful ploys involved stuffing fourteen handker-chiefs into my green KOYLI beret and packing it against my shoulder inside my field exercise denim top. Even so, success was measured by [a] the speed at which my shoulder lost its purple bruised appearance and [b] the swiftness with which my hearing returned to normal on the coach home...

The sheer power of this recoil was best illustrated on the day when we were despatched for the first time ever in groups of six to the 250 yard firing point. Dave Sykes was in our group and he lived for his CCF activities.

Diminutive, wiry and thin as a lath, Syko smoked Woodbines in classic soldier style, gripped between index-finger and thumb, the burning end shielded in his palm. So keen was he to be a soldier that he had also joined the Cadet Force at Batley Drill Hall where he learned his military ways and habits from Regulars and Territorials at the weekends. He could swear using words that we'd never heard of before and he was able to recount

46

vivid tales, gleaned from adult conversations at the weekend camps he often attended, about women's private parts.

Syko knew all about firing .303 Lee Enfield rifles and, as the red flag was duly raised, he swaggers confidently up to the concreted firing point and nonchalantly presses a clip of five rounds live ammunition into the magazine. Along with the rest of us, he spread-eagles himself at number three firing point, all but him dreading the coming twenty rounds' worth of battering from our Lee Enfields. We're given the order to fire the first five rounds at our respective targets and we begin our ordeal.

After each separate shot, I wait expectantly for the cadets in the butts, down behind the protective wall of earth, to raise their eight-foot pointers and indicate whereabouts my shot has penetrated the target [if at all]. Armed with this information, I re-adjust my sights, my firing position and my protective padding, withdraw the bolt and slam home the next round before having another go at the bull. So far so good you think, but what about the recoil? Well, the lesson is learned as we reach the final bit of our shooting session with five rounds "snapshot"...

During this activity, the lads on duty in the butts raise the classic attacking infantryman target above the parapet for a full five seconds. During this time you have to aim and fire at the target. If the cardboard cut-out descends below with a twisting movement - Bingo! - you've killed him. If he waves from side to side - tough luck pal, he's still alive and kicking. But he's only down for five seconds before he rises again during which time, you've to re-load and fire.

Syko and the rest of us are at the ready and the snapshot target is raised. He skilfully closes one eye, aims, gently squeezes the trigger and the crash of the discharge knocks him two feet back on the firing point concrete. Unlike the rest of us who can manage to hold our positions, he is so weedy, he can't stop his puny frame from leaping a couple of feet backwards every time he fires off a round. By the time he's at round number four, we are all in his firing-

47

line because he's loosing off from three yards behind us, and abject terror begins to affect our bodily functions. .303 bullets used to kill Germans, didn't they??? Now, twenty years after the sodding war, we're in danger of being wiped out by one of our own side!

But fear not! Syko has it all under control, despite the fact that the sharp end of his Lee Enfield is waving about like a tree-branch in a Force 9 gale.

"Tha'r awreight," he calls playfully to our cowering, rolled-up-small-so-he-won't-get-us hedgehog shapes. "Just gerrover a bit an' Ahs'll miss thi - Ah've done all this afore, up at Strensall Barracks wi t'fellers. Only one on 'em 'ad to go to t'hospital."

Was I glad to get home in one piece and change my underwear...

*

About a year after escaping with our lives from Dave Sykes and his lethal snapshooting, we were once again aboard a hired coach on our way to the range for a day's ballistic fun with .303 rifles.

Older and much wiser now, I'd made myself a little flannelette cushion of old socks and cotton wool to stuff down my shirt as protection against the Lee Enfield Kicking Mule. Tenderly fondling my protective device in the depths of my small pack, I was actually looking forward to shooting more accurately this time round, possibly earning my "Marksman" .303 badge to sew proudly onto the arm of my battle dress uniform.

Picturing myself scoring maximum points from the 350 yard firing point, I was lost in one of those adolescent reveries way up in the clouds when a sudden and incredulous "Yer bloody what???" brought me back to earth with a thud. It was Lance Corporal Cadet Mike Burgess who was expressing his disbelief. " 'E's bahna do what, d'yer say???"

Lance Corporal Cadet Paul Grafton replied: "It's reight is this - them up theer are up ter summat..." and he indicated some of the Upper Sixth lads at the front of the bus. "Ah've an idea they're tekkin' bets on Horsfall shootin' a sheep when we're up on t'range."

I strained forward, Nosey Parker style, and saw that what Graf was saying was true enough. Money and knowing nods and winks were being exchanged surreptitiously amongst the older lads. By the time we alighted the coach and formed up for the march up the track to the butts, the word was rife throughout the entire Batley Grammar School KOYLI Combined Cadet Force.

The bet had been laid and the conditions agreed: During the final snap-shooting session from the 250 yard firing point, Sergeant Cadet Horsfall was going to plug a sheep - the massive purse of £4-16s-6d being his if the animal was shot dead. [Severe wounding/a complete miss and the bet was off]

Never did a morning's shooting drag on so agonisingly slowly! It seemed that we were all as anxious as each other to arrive at that point in the day when we were in the butts and the older lads were undergoing their final snap-shooting exercise. We anticipated with glee whether or not Horsfall had the "bottle" for the challenge. Opinion was varied as to the outcome of the wager:

" 'E dadn't do it - 'is father'd kill 'im if 'e did"

"What's t'bloody point, eny rooad. Nob'dy'll miss one manky sheep even if 'e does 'it it"

"It's ter bloody far - 'e weeant be able ter see it, ne'er mind kill it"

At last the moment arrived.

The Upper Sixth lads traipsed down to the 250 yard firing point. Those of us who had completed our shoot for the day were lined up behind them with a grandstand view of the coming events. The rest of the detachment went into the butts to perform their duties with pointers, patches and pots of paste, but each and every one of us had but one thought in mind: to gain as good and as clear a sight of the sheep on the far hillside, directly behind the butts, as was humanly possible. As a result, there was an unusual amount of shoving, pushing and jostling immediately behind Firing Point Number Three where Horsfall casually laid down his small pack.

Our Would-be Hero exuded a confident calm as he knelt down on the floor and pressed a clip of five rounds into the magazine of his rifle. There was a grim and determined glint in his eye when he adjusted the sights on his rifle, and I fancy I saw him sneak a furtive glance up the hillside to gauge the distance to his animal target.

An eerie and anticipatory silence fell over the late afternoon scene as we awaited the Officer's command which seemed an age in coming: "In your own time, five rounds rapid......FIRE!"

The snapshot targets appeared over the rim of the butts 250 yards away but the eyes of all the cadet spectators were firmly trained on the far rolling slopes of the green moor. The tiny cotton-wool blobs grazed peacefully in the now-dipping afternoon sun, oblivious to the racket of gun-fire far below. The first salvo of shots ripped through the moor's silence, the targets were lowered and the cotton-wool blobs remained in one piece. A swift five seconds later the process is repeated and still the cotton wool blobs graze on, unaffected by the sound of simulated battle down below.

Murmurs of discontent and cynical mutterings begin to circulate amongst the watchers:

"Ah tell'd thi' - 'e dadn't do it. 'E's chickened aht 'cos 'e's freetened o' gerrin copped."

"Ah berree can't see over yonder - 'e weeant be able ter shoot one if 'is mother's life wor on it..."

By now it's time for the third salvo, and some of the cynics in the audience have lost interest. They turn away and begin their own private conversations. Several of the younger ones begin rummaging in their mess-tins and one or two older lads slope off behind a wall for a "sly swaller". The scenario was beginning to assume the proportions of a severe let-down...

Up came the attacking infantryman once again and the distant count in the butts began, muffled behind the parapet: "One, two, three ....." The salvo rent the air. Up on the hillside, lit dramatically in brilliant sunshine, a cotton wool blob leapt into the air, careered ten feet backwards and crashed over onto the floor. With its legs stiff, straight and pointing skywards it was as dead as next Sunday's joint and ready for the mint sauce...

What discipline we exhibited in the watching ranks! There were no massive cheers of joy or leaps of celebration. Cries of incredulity were stifled and gaping jaws were immediately snapped shut. The most immediate accolades were confined to sly winks or nods. Cadet Corporal "Jock" Sawdon disguised a cry of admiration as a spluttering cough and Horsfall's legendary feat was received in a subdued silence.

The masters [Officers] in charge never tumbled to a thing and their eyes remained firmly fixed on the snapshot targets. We filed past them after the march back to the waiting coaches, and if they'd been alert, they might have detected a hint of glee in our solemn and official declaration as we left the confines of the firing range: "I have no live rounds or empty cases in my possession, sir." Under my breath, I added: "...but I did see Horsfall shoot a sheep and pick up four pound sixteen and a tanner..."

*

One of the dubious joys of being in the CCF was the yearly trek to some far-off barracks on "Annual Camp". On such occasions we met Real-Life squaddies ["Regulars"], lived in Real-Life Nissen huts, slept on Real-Life Army camp-beds and dined on Real-Life NAAFI grub. We came under the watchful, spiteful and beady eye of a Real-Life Company Sergeant Major who was determined to treat us like Real-Life raw recruits. Yes, Annual Camp was a Real-Life experience not to be missed, mainly because you remained safe in the knowledge that all the pain, hardship and Real-Life Army discipline was only for the next ten days!

Now, I don't know about you, but I would have thought

51

that the very last place on earth to take a detachment of *British* Army Cadets from Batley for their Real-Life Annual Camp would be to Northern Ireland! Magilligan Point to be precise - Only a half-decent shillelagh-throw from Donegal in Eire - where the Real-Life IRA lived!!! But that's *exactly* where *we* went in June 1961 at a total cost of 10 bob, all in. So after the rigours of a troop-ship Irish Sea crossing, we arrived in Northern Ireland all prepared for our ten days' worth of Real Army Life...

Reveille was a frightful daily event. I had naively expected it to be heralded by the romantic 06.30 hours bugle-call I'd read about in my comic books, or the "Kiss Me Goodnight Sergeant-Major" of the song "bringing round a nice hot cup of tea". But this was not so.

We were blasted from slumber by the Real-Life CSM running the length of the Nissen hut outside, rattling an iron bar along the corrugated iron sides. The crashing sound only inches away from your head terrorised you out of your adolescent dreams, and the jarring, clattering scrape of metal on metal yanked you, screaming in terror, into the land of the living.

On occasions, some of the lads in my hut were so soundly asleep after the previous day's exertions, and so far into their dreams of having their arms wrapped round Jayne Mansfield or playing alongside Denis Law, that the Magilligan Reveille woke them in abject fright and they lost all control of their bodily functions. The result was a gushing fountain of a good night's urine which drenched the bed in a warm, yellow torrent of terror-induced liquid shock.

But for all the unpleasant memories of Magilligan Camp, there remain at least as many amusing ones - like the running water fights with the lads from the Scarborough College CCF who were also on their Annual Camp; or firing a Sterling sub machine gun - the so-called seven and sixpenny weapon; or, "...just to let you see what it's like...." being subjected to the fire of a section of men [six .303 rifles and a Bren Gun] cowering down beneath the parapet in the butts. This led to yet more terror induced metabolism.

The BGS CCF Company Sergeant Major was [by tradition, of course] an Upper Sixth Former nominated by the masters. At Camp Magilligan, our CSM was the insipid, mealy mouthed creep, McDildough. The CCF Lads-that-Mattered group couldn't stand his greasing ways - he was a teacher's yes-man, always doing as instructed and using his position of authority [CSM] to fend off any danger of physical threat to his creepy well-being.

As you might expect, he got his just deserts when Lance-Corporals Cadets Godbold and Padgett collared him in one of the alley-ways between the Scarborough College Nissen huts, got him down and whipped off his crisply pressed, battle-dress trousers. Throwing open the door of the nearest hut, they slung McDildough in, shouting "'Ere you lot, 'ave some fun with this pillock!"

The animal instinct which was [and is] present in all-male schools came to the surface and the Scarborough College lads immediately recognised the scenario when they espied on McDildough's tunic-arm the three stripes surmounted by a crown, signifying his Very Important Rank.

Cottoning on pretty quickly for private school lads, they bolted the doors at either end of the hut, rugby-tackled the fleeing and terrified McDildough and pinned him to the floor.

In no time at all, they yanked down his drawers and smeared half a tin of Cherry Blossom boot polish thickly and generously round his important bits. Topping off the job with half a jar of really greasy Brylcreem applied with some poor sod's toothbrush, they unbolted the door of the hut a few minutes later and flung out a whinging, wailing, weeping McDildough.

He peered about through his tears, leapt to his feet and, with his well-doctored todger flapping in the breeze, ran all the way back to his own quarters, pursued by hoots of wild derision and a trail of shiny, white Brylcreem blobs on the green Irish grass...

Sometimes we were allowed time off from our official KOYLI duties, and we were given free rein to wander the streets and bars of Portrush and Londonderry in our khaki uniforms. On such occasions, we proudly proclaimed the geographical origin of our regiment to any Irish leprichaun who cared to listen:

"Ey up, sithee...We're fro' Batley, tha knows...." and we would burst into raucous and brash adolescent song at every opportunity:

> *Oh...We're all dahn in t'cellar-oil wheer t'muck slakes on t'winders,*
>
> *We've burnt all us coil an' we're nar burnin' t'cinders,*
>
> *When t'bum bailiff calls, e'll niver find us,*
>
> *'Cos we're all darn in t'cellar-oil wheer t'muck slakes on t'winders.*

And when the natives grunted their Hibernian disapproval, we provided them with a more understandable version which lost a little in the translation:

> *Oh...we're all down in the basement where the dirt accumulates on the casement,*
>
> *We've expended all our coal and we're now burning the ashes,*
>
> *When the privy-councillor arrives, he'll never discover our whereabouts*
>
> *Because we're all down in the basement where the dirt accumulates on the casement.*

During our wanderings around the streets of Londonderry in particular, we pondered, as Batley lads do the world over when they are in foreign parts, why it was that we should receive such meaningful and menacing stares from the shadows of terraced doorways or the dimly lit corners of public bars. It's only from the safety of forty years on that I realise the hatred and scornful disdain in those looks we were given. Even now, I wake from some fitful sleep,

54

with the boney grip of a "Free Derry" Irishman's hand round my clacker in some dark 1961 alley way. The prospect of an explosive device in the hands of a dissident Mick still produces small-hours beads of sweat on my ageing brow.

*

But the real nightmare of Magilligan Point occurred towards the end of our stay in the Emerald Isle. It involved Lance-Corporal Cadet Burgess, RAF Cadet Wild and a remarkable discovery in the grass! This was real brown-underwear stuff and it happened quite by chance on our way back from an exercise in map-reading on the blasted heath and foreshore of the Point, overlooking Lough Foyle and the Republic across the water...

Now, as you might expect, the organisation and smooth running of the BGS CCF Annual Camp [1961] was entirely the responsibility of the teachers - they preferred the term "masters" - that fine body of cultured and intelligent fellows who made up the "Officers" of the CCF. Stiff-upper-lip and all-chaps-together types, _they_ were the daft buggers who had cheerfully sanctioned our afore-mentioned unsupervised meanderings round Londonderry - and they ran absolutely true to form on this occasion...

Despite the fact that various items of serious weaponry had been stolen from the armoury during an IRA raid across the narrow sound of the lough on the previous moonlit night, those officers ordered the said map-reading exercise out in the wilder, wind-swept regions of Magilligan Point. They were utterly oblivious to the fact that the dunes and blasted heath might have been crawling with hysterical Sinn Feiners and Molly Maguires, intent on ripping the innards out of any passing young cadet from Healey, Staincliffe or Batley Carr sporting a British Army uniform!

The actual exercise, however, passed uneventfully into oblivion, and after our day of aimless wanderings on compass bearings, trying to read wind-blasted OS maps, we eventually turned our backs on the bay and headed for Camp, the NAAFI and a nice hot dinner. We shambled back along dry, sandy, well-worn tracks which wove their twisting way through the tall seaside marram grasses, pausing and crouching out of sight now and then for a "sly swaller".

It was on such an occasion, down behind a sand-dune out of sight of the nosey, prying masters, that "Budge" [Lance Corporal Cadet Burgess] made his discovery. There, sitting proudly at the bottom of a low dune, its steely case glinting and winking at us in the late afternoon sun, was a brand new hand-grenade!

Of course, we thought that it was a dummy, left by some squaddies out on exercise weeks ago, so Budge picked it up to look for the blob of paint on the base which would indicate that it was a fake, only used in practice exercises. On discovering that the blob of paint was faded/missing/lost/gone for a walk - in fact had never been there at all - and being a clever bugger from the Grammar School, he immediately jumped to the conclusion that this particular article was "live".

The pin was still firmly in its place on top, the pull-ring shiny and intact, protecting the explosive, destructive capability of the weapon, until some Infantryman Hero yanked it out and "armed" it.

Now you'd think that the first action of any intelligent BGS lad who valued his personal safety would be to swiftly jettison the deadly device with a squawking expletive, dropping it like a red-hot coal from the Nissen hut stove. But not "Budge". Oh no - quite the opposite in fact.

Along with the renowned RAF Cadet Bob Wild, he proceeded to scrutinise the thing like a scientist in a white lab-coat, peering at it and turning it over and over with a view to testing its explosive qualities.

By this time, the brown-trouser factor had begun to have a dramatic effect on the rest of us. We scattered in terror, diving down the side of a nearby dune with our hands together, praying for Divine Intervention as we scrambled for our very lives. I can vividly remember the sick feeling in the pit of my stomach and the beads of cold sweat which erupted from my terrified brow as I spat sand and dry marram grass from my mouth at the bottom of the slope down which I'd bolted along with several others. A few minutes later, in the absence of any explosion, some of us dared to clamber back up and peep over the edge.

"What's up wi' yer - it's reight," shouted Wildy. "It weeant goo off 'cos it's still gorrits pin in - Look..." and he curled his big fat finger through the gleaming ring and swung it round casually, like a PE teacher with his whistle. There were gasps and choked terror-stricken cries behind me and I fancy I even heard the rushing sound of bowel movement near the bottom of the slope.

"Sithee - it's as safe as 'ouses as long as tha dunt pull t'pin," shouted Budge from a safe distance. " 'Ere, give us 'od, Wildy," he demanded as he approached diffidently, attempting to pull rank.

"Thee tek thi time. Get thi mawks off - Ah'm 'avin a reight good look at it," and Wildy proceeded to turn it over in the palm of his meaty hand. In mock terror, he shouted playfully to the rest of us: "It's bloody tickin', man".

There were further gurglings from the bottom of our slope.

" 'Ere y'are, then, Budge. If tha wants it that bad, tha can 'ave it," he said and he tossed it casually, like a fielder at Silly Mid-off, towards the senior ranking man. Budge caught it just as casually and threw it up in the air in celebratory fashion.

By now, amongst the remainder of the group, Discretion had become the greater part of Valour, and we scrambled up the sandy slope, found the zig-zag path in the grass and high-tailed   it in the direction of Camp. From the safety of four hundred yards or so, we paused to check our well-being and the state of our underwear before looking back towards the Crazy Duo.

There they were, sillhouetted against the clear blue sky of the Magilligan Peninsula, throwing this object of destruction back and forth between them like a pair of young day-tripper lasses on the beach at Scarborough. As innocent a scene as you could wish for - except that their "ball" could have blown us all to smithereens in an instant!

From that point on, the incident became the subject of much hearsay. It became a BGS myth that, long after we had bolted for the comparative safety of our Nissen hut where some of the softies had actually dived into bed and hidden under the covers, Burgess and Wild returned to Camp alone, still armed and dangerous. True to their Crazy Cavalier style, they proceeded to use their explosive toy for further amusement amongst the Scarborough College lot....

Of course, there was an innate disdain amongst us Batley lads for any kids who went to a private school, because they were "posh", so any chance to get one up on them was like heaven-sent manna to us - and Burgess and Wild took full advantage of the situation which their "find" now presented. Casually, they ambled down the alley-way between the Scarborough College Nissen huts and, outside the door of the last one, Wildy announced their presence:

"Oi' you in theer - there's two Batley lads 'ere seekin' a feight," he shouted at the top of his voice. "Any o' you posh twats interested?"

There was a long and dramatic pause from inside the hut broken eventually by the sounds of posh lads getting ready for a bout of fisticuffs with those roughies from the Heavy Woollen District.

After a few moments, a door was flung open and out charged eighteen Scarborough College chaps in full dress uniform, growling menacingly and ready for the fray...

"'Cos if y'are," continued Wildy, "tha can try this on for size...." and he rolled the shiny, glinting grenade a few feet along the green Irish turf towards them.

Witnesses say that the eighteen poshies froze in their tracks, gaped at the grenade and immediately experienced the brown-trouser phenomenon. This was later reported in Shoddy Town-speak as "Tha could 'ear 'em shittin' theirsens, man!"

In an instant, the Courageous Eighteen turned tail and dived back into their hut, slamming and bolting the door behind them. Not to be cheated by such an act of cowardice, however, brave Bob reached up to an open window and popped the offending article on the ledge, leering through the glass whilst maintaining one fat finger through the ring-pull. Whinnies of abject terror accompanied the clatter and mad scramble of terror-stricken posh youths as they fought each other to be first out of the door at the opposite end of the hut. The last anyone saw of them, they were disappearing into the setting sun over the dunes of the training area...

Our last sight of the deadly grenade was as Lance Corporal Cadet Burgess lowered it safely and solemnly into a regulation red fire-bucket outside the Scarborough College Nissen hut. "I shall now report this find to our Commandin' Hociffer," he announced imperiously, pulling rank again. He and RAF Cadet Wild then marched off, arguing fiercely.

Wildy maintained that there were many more miles of fun to be had with the grenade if they were to keep their mouths shut and save the weapon until the following day: "We could freeten t'shit out o' some o' t'Regulars in t'NAAFI wi' yond...." were his fading words as the pair strode off up the alley-way between the Nissen huts for the next forty years...

*

The ghost of Captain D.N.R. Lester strides yet again into that dim and distant BGS classroom of yesteryear. The bright afternoon sun glints and dances as it catches his bugle cap-badge and he marches purposefully to the front of the class. He halts and executes a passable KOYLI Right....Turn! ONE, two, three. ONE, two, three; ONE two, three; ONE!

He faces the class and his piercing gaze alights on the greying, balding Would-Be Hero [Second Class] in the front desk.

For the last time, he clears his educated throat with an imperious cough: "Now listen to me ... Are you listening? Good! Now, what I have to say is this: Who is going to join the CCF?"

There is a thick silence and once again, I imagine the averted eyes and the hands in the pockets.

Those words which were never said slice through the silence of the room: "And what about you, Butler? I'm sure you'd enjoy using a field radio in the CCF, wouldn't you?"

"Tha bloody what?" I hear myself reply, incredulously. "Fartin' abaht wi' all that drill an' marchin' an' campin' at week-ends??"

And after a forty-year pause for consideration: "Yes, please, sir! I wouldn't have missed it for the world..."

***

DOPEY DON

The cord-strings of my memory were given a severe yank recently on a sparklingly clear and sunny October day...

It was one of my first jobs as a newly appointed Private-Hire Driver and I was having the time of my life - a Lord of the Road in an eight-seater maroon minibus with wheel-chair access. Sometimes I'd be off to Manchester Airport taking people on their holidays [and there might be a tip - extra bacca-brass!]. On other occasions, I'd be taking the old, infirm and disabled to day-centres or to various council and committee meetings, and the tip would be the advice born of long years of experience: "Tha wants ter get thi cap on aht 'ere, young man, afore tha catches thi deeath...."

On this particular morning, the Boss had called me at nine o'clock and detailed my tasks for the day. "You've a pick-up from a meeting at Batley Town Hall - five OAP's and two wheel-chairs. 15.30 hours."

"Where to?" asks I, always being one for the finer details of a job.

"Eh?....Oh.... er..... They'll tell yer," was the doubtful reply, and the phone clicked dismissively as the Boss hung up.

At the appointed hour, I deftly turned the wheel and entered Batley Market Place to roll to a majestic halt just in front of the stern and sombre facade of the Town Hall. Spick and span, and neatly turned out in jacket and tie, I was new to this job and thought it would be nice for folk to be met by a well-dressed chauffeur - not your usual Saturday night pizza-stained T-shirt wrapped round a ten-foot beer-belly.

I parked up five minutes before the appointed time and made my way up the impressive Victorian staircase to the Committee Room, where the monthly meeting of the Disability Access Group Committee [Batley and Spen

Valley District] had been gathering for their tea and cakes.

I announced my arrival and I was gleefully seized upon by a large, round, red-faced lady who began shouting out names at the top of her brassy voice. One by one, my charges advanced and presented themselves for transport and it slowly dawned on me that I would be spending the next hour or so on the road in the company of several "nutters" - at least, that was what we called them when we were kids.

They were the crack-pots of the Heavy Woollen District - characters who were known and loved by everybody and who lived out their lives in a permanent cocoon of childish oblivion. Their simple minds remained unsullied by the mature responsibility of O-levels and what to take in the Sixth Form. I sometimes envied their naive innocence, as their antics gave us belly-laughs galore in those far-off days - but there was no malice or nastiness in our chortling - we laughed *with* them, not *at* them...

Now, as I ushered today's charges towards my vehicle, I soon discovered that they were all jolly, affectionate, and utterly oblivious to their surroundings as they sailed through life with a big smile and without a care in the world. I came to this opinion as one of the wheelchair-occupiers asked me:"Ey up then, lad! Did yer watch Coronation Street last neet, then? Did yer, eh? Ah 'ad kippers for me tea, tha knows... Ah did! Aye, Ah did that..."

Conversation continued at this sort of level amongst all the occupants of the bus as we loaded up. They talked about toilet arrangements and recent meals, liberally punctuating their remarks with observations, addressed to me, about the person sitting next to them:

"She stinks, 'er... An' she wants ter be first off... Well, she can fiddle if that's what she thinks."

"Are we off up Birstall, mate, 'cos if we are, Ahs'll 'ave ter stop fer a pee..."

"Eee, them cakes they gev us fair med me gip - get me 'ooam afore Ah'm sick..."

But it was Peter Beardsall who crowned proceedings for me with his smiling red face and longish fair hair. I wheeled him up the ramp, clamped his wheelchair to the floor and prepared to shut the rear doors. "Oh," he said in his loud and cheerful manner, "Tha sees 'er in t'front seat?" I nodded confidentially.

"Well, 'alf way through t' meetin', she wet ersen, y'know. She did that.... Peed ersen.... Din't yer, Mary?" he shouted to the front-seat passenger.

I sensed immediately that this conversation might well ruin the harmony and spirit of camaraderie aboard my vehicle. In desperation, I slammed the rear door as noisily as I could and shot round to the driver's seat post-haste, before Mary began to twig that her recent incontinence was about to make headline news aboard my bus.

"Right," says I. "Down to business. Who's going where?" and I turned to look at my charges.

Blank stares all round.

"Where am I taking you," I repeat, slowly, deliberately - and a little louder.

The same blank stares.

Sensing a growing crisis, I decide to ask my chum Peter Beardsall, with whom I felt some rapport:

"Peter! Where are you going...? Where do you live...?"

"Oooh... Nahthen...," replies Peter, sucking in his cheeks and pausing for deep thought. "Erm... Nay, lad... Ah don't know. No, Ah don't," was his sincere reply.

Not to be beaten, I desperately enlist the aid of the other occupants: "Who knows where Peter lives?"

Seven blank stares were my only reply, the silence lasting for what seemed like an eternity. Front-seat Mary starts to mumble and I heave a sigh of relief, sensing help is on hand at last.

" 'E dunt live wi' me - e' lives wi' hissen - an' Ah think Ah need to go to t'toilet, young man..."

Vowing to slot my Boss and resign upon my return to Base, I made my way inside with Mary.

While she busied herself answering Nature's demands, I was able to consult with the large, round, red lady and write myself a hasty list of destinations. By the time Mary and I arrived back at the bus, I was completely in charge and was only too glad to deliver them to their various homes and institutions - Peter Beardsall *et al* - all in one piece!

As I ponder Peter's innocent forgetfulness on the way home from that particular job, the Friday evening rush-hour traffic grinds to an inevitable stand-still. I lean over the steering-wheel of my bus and my thoughts drift away from the diesel fumes and the over-heating press of a hundred waiting vehicles. A mist of time rolls back and as it thins and clears, bright memories of the Nutters of Long Ago come flooding into my cab...

Eric the Fireman is first in - a short, stocky individual with a narrow face, domed protruding forehead, and a yonderly look in his eye. The abiding feature of Eric's appearance was that his neck left his shoulders in a rigid straight line, accentuated by his short-back-and-sides haircut. Well into his thirties, normal life had long since left him far behind. He had no job because he couldn't remember how to do one for much longer than five minutes.

He was "only ninepence to t'shillin'" as the Heckmond-wike locals of the '50s used to say, so every day you'd see him shambling along the streets, aimlessly staring into shop-windows at would-be purchases he could never make. But as soon as that fire-siren sounded at the Fire Station up by the Baths, Eric used to come into his own ...

The siren was a familiar sound to the locals, blasting the peace and calm of the sleepy textile town, threatening to shatter the very glass from the windows. The moment his wing-nut ears picked it up, Eric would turn and dash from one end of the small town to the other, to watch the fire-engine roar into life and clatter its way out of the double-doors in a cacophony of bells and sirens.

He would leap up and down on the pavement outside, a huge grin of joy covering his normally tight and frowning face. He'd wave his arms in the air and shout: "Awreyt, lads? Awreyt, are yer?" and the firemen would wave back as they scrambled aboard their truck, cheerily returning his greeting: "We're champion, Eric - a bit busy reight at this minute, owd lad..."

Now, firemen being firemen and very caring people, they took to Eric after a few fires. Witnessing his excitement and realising they were dealing with a "nutter", they ushered him under their collective wing as a sort of a mascot. He was given a uniform to   wear whenever there was an alert, so from that point on, the scenario changes slightly.

Now, when the clarion call sounds, Eric can be seen tearing the length of Market Street, ripping at his clothing and shouting and gurgling with joy. His jacket, pullover and shirt are left lying on a street-corner and his trousers are often found hanging on the market-square clock, as he races up High Street to dash into the double doors of the Fire Station.

If you were down town shopping and the siren went, you'd see the locals with a knowing look, flatten them-selves against walls or dive hastily for a park bench in the central gardens, anticipating the vortex of Eric the Whirlwind as he tore along Westgate.

Once in the station, he would grab the serge-blue uniform from his personal hook [with its own label] and fiercely start to pull it on. In the early stages, the fire engine would be long-gone by the time Eric got round to doing up his flies, but as time progressed, his dressing skills improved no end.

After a few years, Eric was almost able to sense when the alarm was going to be raised, so that by the time the engine gave out with a mighty rev for the take-off, he would be dressed and ready to go, eager to accompany his fireman-pals on the running-board. No doubt in an effort to slow him down and to avoid his disappointment at not being able to go to the scene of the fire, the lads gave him a veritable pile of equipment to prolong his dressing up - there was even a gleaming fireman's axe complete with buckle-on holster - but such a trick was to no avail.

The more they gave him, the quicker Eric arrived at the klaxon's ring. He could don his kit in the twinkling of an eye, so that eventually, their hand was called, and Eric was "allowed" aboard the big red chariot as it sped to its burning destination.

At the scene, chortling and hopping about, he would stand to one side as the firemen sweated about their life-saving work, and, for some 999 callers, it became a disappointment indeed if Eric failed to turn up on the engine.

"Is Eric wi' yer?" was the earnest enquiry as the fiery blue flames from an unattended chip-pan were expertly doused by the frantic fire-fighters. "'Cos if 'e is, there's a cupper tea for 'im - an' thee, if tha wants one."

Eric the Fireman became a fixture at all the emergencies throughout the locality, jumping up and down and shouting gleeful instructions to the team as the smoke pall of some burning mill billowed higher and higher into the Spen Valley sky ...

There is an irate honk from behind me and I realise that my dreaming has held up the traffic momentarily. I quickly move off and complete all of two hundred yards before temporary traffic lights hold us up again.

The passenger door opens slowly and in climbs Cuckoo. His hair is still receding and greying as it leaps skywards, and his spectacles still perch precariously on the end of his big, red West-country nose - the Sweeper-up from Witney [Oxon] where they make the blankets.

I never knew him by any other name than Cuckoo. He earned his title as a result of *that* trick which was played on him *ad infinitum* by the chaps at P&C Garnett's

[Textile Machinery Manufacturers], Cleckheaton, West Yorkshire, England.

Cuckoo was a labourer - a sweeper-up - fit for no other job than to wheel a barrow about the works, clearing gangways when so-instructed by the fitters and machinists; wielding brush and shovel with amazing dexterity; carrying out his orders to sweep away some metal turnings from beneath a lathe or a milling-machine. A sensible conversation with him was impossible because he prefaced and concluded every remark with the same words in his broad West Country tones:

" 'Course, Oi comes from Witney, y'know - where they d'make blankets - That Oi do.... Oh, yes."

So Cuckoo was fair game for the practical jokers in the factory - and there were plenty of them. You see, Cuckoo was so simple-minded that he would obey any instruction to the letter, no matter who gave it. Take Tarzan, for example. He was a huge bull of a newly-qualified apprentice with a flowing black mane of hair who used to frighten us silly with threats of violence on his return from lunch-time pub visits.

One afternoon, he sidled up to Cuckoo with a mischievous glint in his eye. "Oh, Cuckoo, my mate," he said, oozing false friendship as he put his arm round the Witney man's shoulder.

"This job Ah'm on is very important an' Ah's'll need a barrowful o' smoke for it. Will ta nip darn to t'foundry an gerrus some?"

Cuckoo readily agrees: "Oi will, young man. That Oi will... 'Course, Oim from Witney - where they d'make blankets - Oi am... A barrer load o' smoke... Roight-o!" And off he trots, out of the machine shop and through the big swing doors to the foundry furnace.

It was Tuesday afternoon, so Bill Rigg had just prepared the furnace for lighting. Just before it reached the white-hot casting temperature, clouds of dense, grey smoke billowed from beneath the mighty cupola base, and Cuckoo set to with a will.

He carefully inserts his shovel into the dirty grey clouds and deftly flicks it towards his barrow. After a couple of minutes or so, the Witney man bends over the handles to inspect his handiwork. With a puzzled expression and a scratch of the head, he continues his diligent labour.

Riggy and some of the others couldn't conceal their side-splitting laughter and began to encourage him: "Gi' it some pasty, Cuckoo, owd lad! Goo on lad, shove it inter thi' barrer with thi' 'ands!"

Earnestly attempting to flatten down the smoke in his barrow by hand, Cuckoo laboured on, his face glowing crimson with the unceasing effort and growing frustration. He turned to Riggy: "This bloody stuff won't stay in moi barrer, Bill. 'Course, Oim from Witney, don't yer know, where they..."

"Aye, lad - reight enough," interrupted Bill. "But Ah dooan't think there's goin' ter be enough smoke fer thi' up to press, so tha'd best come back tomorrer..." And with that, Cuckoo gave up the unequal struggle and departed, as the hoots and gales of laughter from the assembled gang of furnace-men drifted after him up the yard.

It was the diminutive Bernard Johnson who let me in on the secret behind Cuckoo's nickname.

One afternoon, I was on my way to the toilet, on the strict orders of the Machine Shop Charge Hand. He had said that I was working too fast and that I'd ruin the job for the rest of them."So tha'd best gerroff for a shit, young 'un..." he'd muttered with a meaningful nod towards the Shop exit door.

Despite my protestations that my constitution was in fine fettle and not in need of purgation, he was adamant, so off I traipsed. I had to pass through the metallic clamour and din of the Fitting Shop where the firm's elite were hard at work.

As employees, fitters were the "*crème de la crème*" because *they* assembled the parts that the rest of us either made or machined, and *they* earned the big money. In the cleaner, lighter atmosphere of their tidy work-bays, surrounded by complicated plans and detailed drawings, they built the working leviathans of the 1960's textile trade. They screwed, hammered and spannered a bewildering array of metal pieces into "Washbowl Willeys" or "Edge Trim Pickers", vital artefacts of the "shoddy" trade on which the Heavy Woollen District thrived.

Soon these shining metal monsters would make their crated way to Newsome's Mill in Batley Carr or to Wormald's and Walkers in Ravensthorpe, where they would grind rags, day on day, month on month, year on year until they could grind no more and the Great Scrap Man from the Sky would claim them for his own.

But right now, demand for the machines was at its height. Because of the need for a great number of parts for this kind of assembly work, the Fitting Shop had an elevated gantry affair around its walls where the vast accumulation of bits and pieces was stored. It was possible to clamber up the steel ladder at the far end of this gantry and survey from on high the wondrous sight of a hundred or so fitters beavering away at their daily toil.

As I passed through, Bernard Johnson, a referee in the local leagues, hailed me, spanner in hand, from the top of a Class A Garnett 20-40: "Nahthen lad...Are ta laikin' a' Sat'day?"

He'd refereed several games in which I'd played so we knew each other quite well. He climbed down from the half-finished machine, ready and eager to idle away a few precious minutes of the firm's time, talking about football in the gangway.

"Aye, Ah am that. We're laikin' Gomersal Mills an' wes'll 'ave us work cut aht, tha can bet."

Just as our conversation is about to develop in detail, who comes along the gangway but Cuckoo, sweeping eagerly and filling his large black wheelbarrow with relish and gusto. He is completely oblivious to his immediate surroundings until Bernard says: "Awreyt, Cuckoo owd lad? Are they keepin' yer busy?"

"Oo ar," replies Cuckoo. "Oi been at it all day, Oi 'ave. Got a fair ole sweat on, Oi 'ave....Oi'm from Witney, y'know, where they d'make blankets. That's roight, Oi am..." and he trundled on his way, sweeping and shovelling.

After Cuckoo had swept and shovelled his way out of earshot, and seeking the answer to a genuine question, I enquired of Bernard: " 'Ow come 'e gets called Cuckoo, Bernard?"

"Dunt ta know? 'Ere, come wi' me an' Ah'll show thi," replies Bernard with an air of confidentiality and hush-hush. With that, he ushers me secretively towards the far end of the shop, up the steel ladder and onto the gantry. From there we have a bird's eye view of the top of Cuckoo's thinning pate in one of the gangways below. Back bent, his eyes are firmly fixed on the sweeping operation in hand.

Bernard peeps over the safety-rail and motions me to get down out of sight as he cups his hands round his mouth.

"Cuckooooo," he trills in a fair copy of the bird's call, and he swiftly ducks out of sight, behind the rail. Cuckoo immediately looks up from his work and responds in like vein.

"Cuckoo! Cuckoo!" he chortles delightedly, his face abeam with a massive ear-to-ear grin. He peers round the fitting-bay, earnestly searching for his rustic roots. In his mind, he is gambolling along some Oxfordshire country lane in the spring sunshine.

Still hidden, but peering through the gaps in the railing, Bernard and I are convulsed with boyish glee. After waiting for a crest-fallen Cuckoo to return to his sweeping-up, Bernard gives it another go, but this time with a far more realistic impression: "Cuckoo!" And once again, Cuckoo responds, hopping up and down the aisles nodding his beak like the very bird itself and calling with all his Witney-might; "Cuckoo! Cuckoo! Cuckoo!"

Bernard and I continue in secret and silent mirth until Witney Man has "cuckooed" himself to exhaustion and he

dejectedly abandons his search. He returns to his wheelbarrow as his Oxfordshire lane sadly wilts, fades and
drifts away on a breath of nostalgic air, disappearing into
some cranny of the simpleton's brain - gone but not
forgotten...

I climb down the steel ladder and amble off down the
long gangway of time-gone-by and back to the present.
The traffic lights have changed and my file of vehicles
moves slowly on its way. The cab has become stuffy after
the five minutes' stand in traffic so I inch down the
driver's window and look idly down at the pavement.

There, holding his hand out to stop the bus, is my
childhood's Nutter of Nutters - Dopey Don.

Throughout the Shoddy Towns of the 50's and 60's,
everybody knew Don and his antics. Well into his thirties
and dressed in his green school blazer and green school
cap, his boney white knees stuck out from the hems of his
regulation grey short trousers. With buck-teeth and an
elderly face, it was not so much his appearance that
endeared him to the locals but rather his mode of
transport.

Don was the proud owner of a scooter. No, it wasn't one
of those Lambretta jobs so popular in the 60's. This was a
proper push-as-you-go scooter - the one-foot propelled
affairs beloved by generations of kiddies. Don would leg
his scooter the four miles from Birstall Market Place to
Dewsbury Town Hall, cheerily waving to all and sundry
whether he knew them or not. "Awreyt, mister," he'd
shout, in between his impersonation of a 650 Norton
motor-bike engine. "Awreyt, are yer?"

"Aye, I am that, Donald," was the inevitable friendly
reply.

But most impressive of all was the limber-work of the
scooter. It was festooned with badges of all sorts - AA,
RAC, Pony Club of Great Britain to name but three. The
handle-bars had been specially made to enable Don to
carry a net-bag full of footballs on the left and an ornate
hand-operated horn on the right. Bits of chrome had been

fitted to the sides of the vehicle and, all in all, Don presented a Quixotic image as he travelled the length of Bradford Road, his green cap fixed firmly in place and the summer sun glinting and dazzling as it caught the chrome fairings of his trusty steed.

We used to see Don regularly at the bottom of Carling-how Hill when school was out and we were waiting for the bus home.

He would often park his scooter next to the wall behind the bus- shelter and join us in the queue.

"What yer doin', lads?" asks Don, enthusiastically.

"Waitin' for t'bus 'ome, Don. Ar' yer waitin' wi' us, then?"

"Aye - Ah'm waitin' for t'A bus to Thornhill," and at that moment, the "A" bus from Birstall [Market Place] to Thornhill [via Dewsbury] hoves into sight. Don is overcome with joy and he starts hopping up and down on the spot and gurgling with delight.

Dashing to the front of the queue, he extends his left arm as the bus draws near. With a serious expression on his face, he rests his forehead on his outstretched arm and cocks his right eye expectantly in the direction of the on-coming bus.

The driver has spotted a passenger, so he heaves-to at the stop and the open platform at the back draws to an accurate halt opposite Don.

"Are yer gerrin on, then?" the conductor asks, his right hand resting on the cranking handle of his silver-grey ticket machine. After a pause for thought, Don delivers his verdict: "Nar...." and he shakes his head vigorously.

The conductor sighs, looks heavenward and irately but crisply dabs the bell-push beneath the stairs to the upper-deck. The tinkling sound has hardly died away in the driver's cab before the "A" bus revs noisily and trundles off on its smokey deisel way to Thornhill [via Dewsbury] Don smiles, returns to his scooter and rummages aim-lessly in the net-bag of footballs on the handle-bars. Next along is the Number 4 bus [Bradford - Dewsbury via Birstall] and once again, Don is excited.

The process of hailing the bus is repeated with every bit as much enthusiasm, but this time there is a slight variation in the resulting conversation:

"Are yer gerrin on, then?"

"Is this a 4 bus," asks Don.

" 'Course it is - it says so on t'front, dunnit? Well - are yer gerrin on?"

Pause for thought... "Nar..." with an earnest and vigorous shake of the school-capped head.

Such a scenario was a regular occurrence at that particular bus-stop [and no doubt at many others across the Shoddy Towns], but throughout my scholastic youth, I never once saw a conductor lose his temper or curse at Don. The locals - we school kids included - revered him and treated him as a sort of Heavy Woollen District icon, deserving of our respect and not our derisory laughter. He was famous the length and breadth of Dewsbury and Batley, and it was almost as if you were courting doom and ill-fate if ever you laughed at Don...

It's a Wednesday morning in spring and the market-folk have been hard at work since dawn, loading up their stalls and emptying their vans. As the sun shines down on Long Causeway and the Town Hall clock strikes ten, Our Hero is burning up the pavement [and the sole of his right shoe] as he weaves his way at breath-taking speed through the covered market. He's not stopping to buy today because he's on a far more important mission.

"Ey up, Don," shouts Clem from the "Dewsbury Surplus" stall. "An' wheer dusta think tha'r off ter?"

" 'Ospital," replies Don. "Ah've bust me leg ageean!"

And he right-legs it onto Cloth Hall Street and up Halifax Road towards Dewsbury General Hospital.

Twenty minutes later, Don is wearily legging up the leafy drive of the General Hospital, breaking off at the roundabout in front of the Victorian archway-entrance to whizz round three or four times making 650 Norton noises.

After parking up his machine in a spot marked "Doctors Only", he dashes into Casualty and knocks furiously on the small window at the start of a long, black and white checkered marble-floored corridor. The window slides back to reveal the white-capped head of the Sister-in-Charge.

"Now then, Donald....What's up today, love?"

"I've bust me leg ageean - laikin' football last neet," is Donald's succinct explanation, whereupon Sister invites him to go down the corridor to the door on the right...."where we'll see to it for you."

Five minutes later, Don is once again mobile, zooming around the roundabout, impersonating the 650 Norton, with a large "Elastoplast" round his finger.

"There y'are, Donald," the young nurse in Casualty had said. "This bandage'll sort your broken leg for you, won't it" and she'd tenderly wrapped his finger in sticky plaster. Donald had accepted the medical advice without question, vigorously nodding a grateful beam of thanks...

Association Football was the love of Don's life.

He was never without his net-bag containing three or four footballs, carefully slung over the handle-bars of his scooter. Whenever a game was in progress and Don happened to be right-legging it past, he would park up, watch for two or three minutes and then proceed with his own version of the Beautiful Game.

I last came across him when I was playing for Old Batelians on Sands Lane fields in the late 60's

Our game had been well under way for about twenty minutes on Pitch Number 3 when, turning idly in my goal because play was down the other end, I noticed the school-capped and blazered figure scooting out from underneath the sombre arches of the railway line and onto the area behind my goal. He downed his scooter and knelt

"An' wheer dusta think tha'r off ter?"
" 'Ospital ... Ah've bust me leg ageean!"

to rummage in his net-bag. By the time I'd dealt with the opposition's next attack, Don's personal game was in full swing.

He'd taken out his footballs, whistle and linesman's flag and gone over to the empty goal of the adjacent Pitch where he proceeded to play an important Cup Tie versus Himself.

This required him to assume a complete set of different rôles:

1. Home team players 2. Away team players
3. Referee   4. Linesmen
5. Home supporters   6. Away supporters

From a distance of some forty yards or so, I could see him kicking the ball the length of the pitch, chasing after it and shouting words of encouragement to himself.

At one point, he crashed to the turf as if felled by a crunching tackle. Appealing vociferously to the referee [himself], he hauls himself back onto his feet, flicks the greasy mud from his knobbly knees and chases the ball all the way back to the goalmouth from which he had started.

He copied snatches of language gleaned from touchlines other than the Yorkshire Old Boys' League as he proceeded to alternately encourage and berate himself for the performances of all concerned in his own private game:

Picking himself up from the muddy surface of Sands Lane Pitch Number 4a after yet another long chase the length of the field and a fairly dramatic fall, the dialogue with himself runs roughly as follows:

"Yer dirty bastard - that were a bloody foul" [Home team player]

"No it worn't, yer daft twat" [Away team player]

"Yer must be bloody' blind, ref! 'Ee were a bloody mile off-side then" [Home team supporter]

"Wor 'e 'eck!" [Away Team supporter]

The whistle sounds as Don trots to the touchline: "Did you see if he wor off-side, then?" [Referee]

A vigorous nodding of the head and waving of the flag: "Off-side!" [Linesman]

A blast of the whistle: "Right! Free-kick - just 'ere." [Referee]

The free kick is taken and Don [Home Team player] hares off after the ball, shouting encouragement to himself. He kicks the ball through the far goalposts, leaps in the air, chortling, cheering, yelling, somersaulting and roaring the roar of a thirty thousand crowd...

I stand in my goalmouth of yester-year, hands on hips and watch.

Slowly and eerily, two shadows creep from beneath the arches away to my right and join Dopey Don. Wielding a glinting fireman's axe, Eric the Fireman dashes urgently towards Pitch Number 4a, followed at a leisurely shamble by Cuckoo, brandishing a sweeping-brush. They look as if they are about to join him in his ghostly kick-about as they dance and leap towards him, but the piercing blast of our full-time whistle shatters the tranquillity of my part-time dream.

I turn to congratulate my team-mates, and when I look back over my shoulder, the three of them have gone.

They've disappeared forever under the bridge, back to a time when the cobbled streets of Dewsbury and Batley were still cobbled, Taylor's mill-chimney still belched thick, black smoke and "*The Shoddy Towns*" featured in Geography text-books the world over.

***

MUFFITT'S LAST STAND

It was a cold, grey November afternoon in 1952. I poked my nose through the stern, black ironwork of the railing near the Meadow Lane players' tunnel and strained to catch a glimpse of the legendary Tommy Lawton as he took the field for the Magpies. Just after noon on that momentous day, my Dad had donned his trilby, pocketed his packet of twenty Player's Navy Cut, carted me onto a Barton's Bus and taken me off to his spiritual home. After shoving me down to the front of the main stand past thousands of over-coated and flat-capped people, he informed me imperiously that I was watching Notts County v Nottingham Forest...

I remember it as if it was yesterday. I was frozen stiff and unable to move a muscle, jammed up against the cold steel of the railings by the knees of dozens of giant blokes. There was the dank vapour of cigarette detritus and stale pee rising from the floor - and it was a 0-0 draw.

Already, football had taught me a lesson for life. From that moment, I vowed that I would actively *play* the game rather than become a passive watcher of the professionals. Not for me the freezing cold of the Saturday afternoon terraces, the comforting warmth of the smokey top-deck on the bus home or scrambled eggs for tea. No - those were the week-end distractions of Old Codgers. I was going to play the game at the highest level - for Wolverhampton Wanderers or the Arsenal or Notts County .... and England.

Everybody in the whole wide world - regardless of colour, creed or sex - should be *made* to play football. Regular participation in the Beautiful Game would improve the state of humanity no end. Where else can you learn to accept the decisions of others whilst practising the art of self-control; to live with the failings and foibles of your fellow human-beings; to take Life's triumphs and disasters on the chin; or to lovingly share changing-room and bath with dozens of other people? By playing football, of course! Not the professional fiasco which masquerades as a sport and which you see on the telly *ad nauseam* these days. No - to get the best out of the Beautiful Game, you need to play as an amateur at a fairly modest level. That's where the *real* lessons for life are to be learned...

Ever since I alighted from my nappies, football has always played an important part in my life. Not that I was ever any good - College First Team Captain was the pinnacle of my success - and that's because at Goldsmiths' College, London in the mid-60's, the women outnumbered the men by three to one. Anyone who could kick a ball more than six yards and who was able to see across a public bar to order three pints after the match was guaranteed a game. Besides, many of the most promising footballers amongst the students were heavily involved in another sport, known locally as "nadging".

But the idea of competing sportingly on the football field was one that always appealed to many lads of my generation. By running round semi-naked on freezing Saturday afternoons, caked in foul-smelling mud and streaked with the sweat of honest toil, we came to learn all there is to know about the finer things in Life. Like that time one winter at the age of thirty-something, I was gracing the field for Wheelwright Old Boys in a West Riding County Cup game in Hull...

We were seven-nil down and had been given the run-around all afternoon by a far superior team. Five minutes remained of the tie and the withering East Coast wind was blasting at us straight off the North Sea, carrying its load of hail and ice-spicules to cut and rip our bared flesh. Frozen shorts were chafing our reddened thighs and we were all longing for the final whistle and a hot bath to ease the pain. But did we give up the valiant struggle?

In his own typical style, Skipper Never-Say-Die/Never-Beaten-Till-The-Final-Whistle Dr. Frank Goodall [Vice-Principal, Salford College] exhorts us to make one last supreme, super-human effort. Through gritted teeth, his stentorian tones ring loud and clear through the howling wind and hail: "Come on, Wheelwright! We can still do it!"

As a man, we turn to our courageous Skipper in the true sporting tradition of the Yorkshire Old Boys' League. We stick out our chests, fill our lungs to capacity and deliver our heroic response: "Oh, f... off, Frank."

Long, long before that particular incident, I made my competitive footballing debut for Dogsthorpe Primary School at the age of nine.

For eager weeks before, I'd gorged myself on the photographs in my Charlie Buchan's 1953 Book of Soccer, and I'd noted the poses struck by my footballing heroes: Billy Wright [Wolverhampton Wanderers], Raich Carter [Hull City], Leon Luty [Notts County], Len Duquemin [Tottenham Hotspur]. Beneath a plastered mat of thickly Brylcreemed locks with straight tram-track partings, all had eyes firmly fixed on a distant ball having just kicked it. All my heroes held one arm aloft, pointing in the general direction of the kick, the other pointing behind them at the turf. All of them had a steely determined look on their serious gritty faces. *This* was how proper footballers played the noble sport.

So on the morning of the match, I raided Dad's Brylcreem jar and buttered my scalp so as to plaster my hair firmly to my skull, ready for the coming fierce encounter. After an interminable and agonising morning of Arithmetic and Spelling, I took to the field in the afternoon as Leon Luty, Len Duquemin, Raich Carter and Billy Wright - the very embodiment of footballing perfection.

Throughout that baptismal game, I struck the poses of my heroes, holding my statuesque manifestations, tableau-like, long after the ball had gone, echoing the 1953 Book of Soccer photographs which I'd committed to memory. Play passed me by, back and forth; kids shouted at me and teachers on the touch-line implored me to move about. But I remained stock-still, one arm aloft, pointing in the general direction of my kick, the other pointing behind me at the turf. I was playing for England at Wembley, defending *our* style of football against Ferenc Puskas and his nancy-boy Hungarians - every inch a modern footballer.

After such an impressive and successful debut, I was utterly baffled when Mr Nicholls, our teacher, failed to select me for the subsequent game: v Stanground Primary in the local Schools' Cup.

Instead of gracing the green sward, I was given the serious responsibility of guarding Class Four's bank-money in the teacher's desk drawer while the rest of the kids went out to watch. I spent the entire game in the hollow silence of an empty classroom, sitting alone at the front and muttering to myself: " I 'ope they lose bi six goals...an' I 'ope the bloody cross-bar drops on Mr Shitty Nicholls' 'ead..."

Just after this, my footballing career came to a temporary halt. As a result of my dad's quest for better employment, I ended up at a grammar school in Stroud where they played Rugby Union.

Referred to by Wally [Mr Waldron] the PE teacher, as "football", this has got to be one of the craziest games ever invented. Brute strength and hugely over-developed neck-muscles are seemingly the only requirements for success. As soon as one poor sod gets the ball and tries to make progress up the field, everybody else jumps on him, wrestles him to the ground and tries to kick the living shit out of him - including his own team.

Just after that, the referee blows his whistle and we start all over again. This time, we crouch down facing each other and earnestly endeavour to shove our opponents backwards, even before the oddly-shaped ball has been chucked into the tunnel between us.

So there I am, in the front row of a House Match, earnestly straining my gut and heaving with all my puny eleven-year old might, when I feel an agonising and grinding stab of pain in my left thumb. At the break-up of the scrum, I tenderly nurse the injured bit in my other

81

hand and discover that some lousy bastard has bitten it - right down to the bare white bone which is winking up at me right next to a purple blob of blood. I gingerly replaced the flap of skin, squashed it down - and fainted.

"Bugger this for a game of soldiers," says I to myself, vowing *never* to be caught with or without the ball in that nasty scrum *ever* again, and I make like a rat from a trap for the comparative safety of Right Centre. Playing there, I find that I can exercise my considerable passing skills as soon as any member of the opposition approaches within five yards of me.

Such skills, along with a liberal dose of cowardice and a very sore thumb, ensured my survival for the next few months until my Dad got himself another job. This meant a move to Yorkshire - to a *proper* school playing *proper* football.

By now, the greatest footballer ever to grace a field had arrived in Heckmondwike at the age of 16. He'd played his first game for Huddersfield Town Juniors and had already been thrust into First Team, Second Division, action. It was, of course, the slight, blond-haired, bespectacled Hero of our adolescence - Denis Law.

After playing school matches on Saturday mornings, I forsook my erstwhile life-long vow never to become a spectator and took to the Popular Side at Leeds Road to watch Huddersfield Town. Along with Dick Perkins, "Wonger" Nixon and one or two other chums, I gazed fortnightly on our footballing heroes in action.

Managed by Bill Shankly, the likes of Big John Coddington, Ray Wilson and Les "Streaker" Massie strutted their stuff, but none could match Denis's charismatic skill. His brilliance on the ball took our collective breath away. His slide-rule accurate passing was often lost on his slower, less perceptive team-mates. His goal scoring and right arm aloft celebration were pure joy.

However, Denis's most outstanding and awe-inspiring attribute, marking his superiority over all others, was the way he held his shirt-sleeves!

You see, he gripped his sleeves at the cuffs and held them over his hands for the entire ninety minutes of every game I saw him play. Holding his arms bent at the elbow, away from his body, he produced the characteristic Law pose which came to be feared throughout the World during his whole career.

As you might expect, we all copied his style of play along with those characteristic gestures. Witness any game of proper football at Batley Grammar School in the early 60's and you'd see ten* carbon copies of Our Denis, all gripping shirt-cuffs, arms akimbo, laying slide-rule passes with a bob of the head whilst tear-arsing round the school pitches of the West Riding.

By this time, I had taken stock of my playing abilities and had decided that, as a skillful right-half in the Billy Wright mould, I was next to sod-all use. So, desperate to play football, I became a goalkeeper.

Quite content with my lot, I was making regular appearances with the school Second team in the morning and had begun to fancy my chances of guarding the sticks for Hightown Youth [Heavy Woollen Minor League] in the afternoon. But then fate took a hand in determining my career - in the shape of Geoff Wharton, the Hightown manager - and my Dad.

You see, diminutive, flat-capped Mr Wharton ran Hightown Youth FC. From his council house on Windy Bank Estate, he did *all* the mugging about necessary to field a side of under-18 lazy buggers.

He attended League meetings, organised a pitch, hired changing facilities in the Scout Hut behind the Brown Cow, ran training sessions on Thursday evenings and begged sawdust from Joe Bland's Timber merchants for marking out our Miry Lane pitch. The man was a selfless hero. So it was only fair, in view of the fact that Geoff did

---

*   Only ten, even though a proper football team has eleven good men and true. Goalkeepers found it extremely difficult to emulate the style of Our Hero without jeopardising their chances of selection for the following week.

all the donkey-work, that his son, John, should play every week - which he did - in goal.

This forced Yours Truly into a drastic career-change, reverting to my role as intelligent, scheming wing-half. But it meant that I came under the scrutinizing eye of my father on a weekly basis because Dad, along with one or two others, had "volunteered" his services to help Mr Wharton in the management and selection of the team. As far as I was concerned, it meant that I played out under his hypercritical gaze every sodding Saturday!

As you might expect, I had to endure severe touch-line criticism and jibes from some of the estate kids who didn't get into the team.

"Well, tha'r ner bloody good, thee. Tha only gets a game 'cos thi father picks t'team," was a familiar insult at Thursday night training sessions when the team-sheet went up on the Scout Hut notice-board. But I sensed that my days as a successful right-half were numbered one dull November afternoon as the gathering dusk began to descend on our Miry Lane efforts to progress to the next round of the area cup...

We were a goal down and had been floundering our way through the rain-sodden treacle surface for about eighty minutes. From out of the gloom somewhere in the far reaches of the bottom touchline, Dad's Stentorian voice boomed from the shadows,

"Come on, Fred, lad! You're running about like a bloody great cart-horse!" My watching critics fell about laughing before making neighing sounds from behind our goal.

A few weeks after, I departed for a local works' team in the open-age league to play in goal...

Now, even though I say it myself, as time progressed, I became quite a decent 'keeper. I'd replaced "Flash" Quick in the school First Team and I was playing regular open-age football in the local league on Saturday afternoons. I was "watched" by both Arsenal and Wolves scouts and I'd begun to fancy my 18 year-old's chances for that coveted career in football.

But just as I was beginning to feel that things were going my way, along comes a player in the shape of Big Jack Charlton to fill me in on the truth of the matter...

At the three grammar schools in our locality, during the Christmas holiday break, the County Football Association ran five-day coaching courses for budding young sixth-formers. It was on one such course that we met the great man himself - but in those far-off days, he was a newly-qualified FA Coach playing centre-half at Leeds United. His heady summer triumphs of 1966, when he fell to his knees at the end of extra-time, were still some three years in the future.

For the present, he ran our coaching sessions in several cold, draughty, Shoddy Town gymnasia.

Now, as football followers the world over will verify, Big Jack has never lost his endearing North-East accent, and the knottiest problem for we Shoddy Town lads was interpreting the great man's instructions to us in his sincere efforts to improve our playing abilities. Often carried away by his own enthusiasm, Jack's Geordie twang was as good as a foreign language to us as we stood, open mouthed after a Charlton pronouncement.

During one session on shooting, Jack sums up in his own tongue and proceeds to the next stage of the coaching exercise: "Right lads, that was champion. Noo, Ah need a goolie*..."

Believing amongst us that we were on to a scandal of newspaper proportions ["Leeds United defender lacks vital body-part"] and not knowing how to respond, we stared at each other in gob-struck amazement.

At this, Jack gets somewhat aerated.

---

* Goolie schoolboy slang for a testicle. viz: During a game of *proper* schoolboy football, the following cry was often heard after a particularly violent clash between body and ball: "'E'll be reight in a minute, sir. 'E's nobbut copped one in t'goolies."

* Goalie old fashioned terminology for the guardian of the goals in a *proper* football match

"Come on, lads - a goolie..... Which one of ye's plees in gool for yer bloody school team, like?"

Pent up sighs of relief echoed round the school gym. Jack *wasn't* missing an important bodily part and I was so over-joyed that I volunteered immediately for shooting practice. Every time my body hit the floor, Jack bellowed his FA Coaching Manual encouragement at me: "C'mon, goolie! Gerrup on yer feet, man!"

The climax of that week's coaching was an awe-inspiring visit to Leeds United's Elland Road ground and a full game against their Junior side. [Jimmy Greenough and Billy Bremner both played; Jack graciously made up their numbers] But we were too gob-struck to concentrate on football. Shoddy Town lads, *playing* at Elland Road. To us, it was like a dream.

After the game, fawning and greasing like hell, we thought to advance our football careers by asking Jack if we might be allowed to thank Don Revie for allowing us the privilege of using the Elland Road facilities. The Big Man readily agreed, and we filed reverently into the office of another footballing legend - the architect of the Deep-Lying Centre Forward and the perpetrator of the Revie Plan.

We respectfully thanked him, but as the words came out of our mouths, our Shoddy Town thoughts were totally dominated by the notion that we were talking to *the* Don Revie who would eventually occupy *the* top job in English football.

So enthralled by such thoughts were we, that we almost missed the significance of the Don's reply to us. He invited us to contact him at any time in the future, after our studies had been completed, if we were interested in a career in football! We came out of that office on Cloud Nine.

The Leeds United manager had made us an offer of professional status.

But Big Jack brought us all back down to earth with a resounding thump.

"Nar..., " he said, shaking his head. "You lads'll never be pros as long as ye's've hools in yer arses - an' d'ye's know why?"

Our shoulders drooped and we shook our heads in dejected fashion.

"Well, Ah'll tell ye's. Ye's'll never play football fer yer bread an' butter, ye' see, so ye's'll never have the killer instinct to win at all costs. Ye's'll always earn yer livin' doin' somethin' else - so just enjoy yer football, lads, an' forget all aboot the money."

It was devastating news at the time, but the Big Man was absolutely right, as he was about most things during his long, illustrious footballing career.

My "career" lay in the lower reaches of amateur football and, as promised, it taught me a great deal about the finer things in Life. After a week's gruelling toil to earn an honest crust at the chalk-face, there came the welcome week-end release onto the football fields of the West Riding.

Like over-sized schoolboys, we'd bare our flesh and spend Saturday afternoons floundering and cavorting in mud. We'd drink vast quantities of beer after the game, and spend the evening on a settee snoring in a drunken stupour. And the lessons for Life lay in the characters I was privileged to meet and the events I was lucky enough to witness...

In the Spen Valley League, Division Two, Season 1961-62, local football displayed some of its more mundane characteristics. Before taking the field for a 3pm kick-off, many of the footballing gladiators who played for P & C Garnett's Ltd had already completed a morning's overtime [time-and-a-half]. Now, after clocking off, what could be more pleasant than to repair to "The Punchbowl" at the top of Stone Street for liquid sustenance until closing time [2.30pm]? This would leave just enough time to return to the works shower block - which were now our Saturday afternoon changing-rooms - and prepare for the coming encounter. As a young player with aspirations [despite

Big Jack's previous words of wisdom], I never joined in with this quaint custom, still taking my football seriously.

How well I remember my first game for the works' side!

I'd played reasonably well in goal throughout the first half, encouraged by Skipper Billy Ramsbottom, a craggy ex-pro with Chesterfield. As the half-time whistle sounded, I collected my cap and gloves from the back of the net and trotted eagerly up to the half-way line for the team-talk.

By the time I arrived, Joe Loughran, foundry foreman from Belfast, was already there. He'd only recently taken to wearing a jock-strap in which to play and had been heard on many occasions during a game rapturously praising his new purchase: "Jeez, this is a wonderful piece of equipment, so it is. Stops yer tackle swingin' about inside yer shorts, so it does."

On this occasion, however, Joe, like some of the others, was bouncing up and down on the spot, hopping from one foot to the other, inhaling deeply and eagerly rubbing his hands together. He was obviously keen and anxious to begin the second-half, I thought.

"Gather round, lads," instructs Skipper Billy. "Get round 'ere and listen up..." I join the tight-knit circle of blokes in their black and gold kit, eagerly anticipating a serious session on playing style and tactics from the gritty old professional footballer.

Billy clears his throat and announces to his eleven: "Joe's bustin' for a piss an' there's a woman on t'touchline..."

So we made our circle round Joe who outs with his tackle and relieves himself bang on the centre-spot. Several others of the Punchbowl Set felt a similar need and responded in like vein, thus drenching that very important part of the pitch-markings. It was a noticeable feature of the game from then on that most of the players from both sides took great pains to avoid that area of the centre circle which was still giving off clouds of acrid vapour late into the second half...

But it was in the Yorkshire Old Boys' League where I learned that football was still being played in true halcyon style. In such a league - and there were many around the country - the game was played by intelligent players who were clever enough to know how to play skillful football, but who generally lacked the physical adeptness to do it!

The end result, for me at any rate, was a series of weekly experiences which I wouldn't have missed for all the beer in Tetley's Leeds brewery...

Playing for Old Batelians one dull afternoon in March, 1963, I was privileged to take part in the notorious Keith Muffitt's very last game for the club. By now well into his thirties, Keith was a tall, stocky rock of a centre-half who had also opened the bowling for Gomersal Cricket Club during his summer months away from the football field.

Not of a very violent nature, despite it being a fine quality for a stocky centre-half/opening fast bowler to possess, Keith found it extremely difficult to tolerate injustice of any kind. He had made the lead article in the local newspaper [complete with photograph] following a bizarre incident involving a cart-load of farmyard manure...

The local farmer had been muck-spreading in the field behind Keith's house. In addition to the discomfort of the foul smell pervading the tranquil air, some of the offensive material had been flying from the spreader and landing in gardens bordering the field, thus upsetting the residents. Despite appeals from the house-owners, the ruddy-faced and obstinate farmer continues his agricultural practice for several days.

At this point, Keith decides he can take no more.

Approaching the farmer diffidently, he politely requests that the tractor and muck-spreader be driven closer to the middle of the field, thus reducing the range of the flying dung. The farmer delivers a succinct agricultural refusal, wherupon Keith plucks him bodily from the seat of his vehicle and flings him deftly into the freshly loaded manure trailer.

All of which brings us to that dull March afternoon of Muffitt's Last Stand...

Keith was once again occupying the Old Batelians number five shirt, having done so for several years, but in this particular side, his gritty, determined defensive play had been influential in keeping us on top of the league for most of that season. Today, we were playing Old Hansonians from Bradford, who were renowned for their art of winning at all costs. Knowing ones would call this "cheating", but this was the Old Boys' league where such activities were dishonourably taboo, so they must be referred to as "gamesmanship".

Yours Truly had had the most inactive season to date. The 'keeper in a successful side has little else to do other than flit between the posts in a never-ending series of bodily contortions in the effort to keep warm. In mid-January I'd considered asking our Skipper if I might take a hot-water bottle and a flask of rum into the net with me, but had abandoned the idea for fear of the unceasing piss-taking which might have resulted in the showers after each game. But now it was Hanson, and we all knew that we'd have to be on our mettle to avoid defeat by "gamesmanship".

As expected, they were at it from the kick-off. The Old Hansonians centre-forward - a callow youth in his mid-twenties - was up to some artful tricks. In every aerial tussle with Muffitt, he would fall to the floor with exaggerated and dramatic gestures, making loud, plaintive appeals to the referee: "Pushin', ref! 'E's at it all t'time!"

But of course, like all referees this particular Man-in-Black is an intelligent and discerning human-being, able to make fair and balanced judgements about all the scenarios with which he is confronted on the field of play. Does he see through the theatrical efforts and gamesmanship of the Hansonian cheat? Does he note the uncomplaining diligence of our Keith to get on with the game? Does he quietly warn the callow youth that his amateur dramatics have failed to create an impression? Does he chuff!

Instead, he swallows the bait [whole] every time, and free-kick after free-kick is awarded against the honest, hapless Muffitt.

However, no gain is made as a result of such cunning Hansonian ploys, and at half-time, there is no score.

We spent the interval muttering dire threats about the centre-forward's immediate future [a canal ran alongside the pitch]. We questioned his very parentage and we christened him "Oscar" as a sincere tribute to his acting ability.

At length, after slaps on the back all-round, we took the field for the second half, thoroughly resolute in our desire to win fairly and squarely. However, events overtook us somewhat, about fifteen minutes after the re-start.

Oscar had resumed Act Two and the dramatics continued as free-kicks were awarded against us, when there was yet another aerial duel between Oscar and Keith. Muffitt rises majestically and heads clear while our Hansonian charlatan crashes to the floor and begins his display of thespian talent.

On this occasion, we are treated to a dramatic performance of outstanding merit as Oscar lets forth such a convincing yell of anguish that we are certain someone has introduced a very large, white-hot foreign body into his rectum. He falls to the earth with a slap like a felled oak, clutching his head and writhing in fake agony. Several of us marvel at such a confident performance in one so young, and there is a small ripple of polite applause. But we are soon shaken out of such an appreciative mood when the referee's whistle pierces the air and the Man-in-Black moves menacingly towards Muffitt.

"That's it, number five. I've had enough! I've warned you five times, so now you're off - go on!" He points imperiously towards the touchline where the players' tunnel would have been if we'd been at Wembley. Puffing out his chest, he delivers his haughty command: "You will now leave the field of play."

91

Keith was flabbergasted. "You're not sendin' me off, are yer, ref? I never touched 'im...."

"Yer've bin kickin' seven colours o' shite out o' t'poor sod since t'kick-off, so off yer pop," replied the Man-in-Black flicking a derisory thumb over his shoulder in the general direction of the imaginary players' tunnel.

With appealing looks all-round, Keith resigns himself to his fate and troops off towards the touchline, outwardly dejected; inwardly seething. Like the rest of us, he noticed the sly, secretive smiles on Hansonian faces and Oscar's smug grin, but he reaches the touchline and stands in silence for a while, contemplating his next move.

Play was continuing at the other end of the field when Keith announced to all those present his carefully considered course of action: "Well...if Ah'm bein' sent off, Ah might as well be sent off fer doin' summat."

He spun dramatically on his heel and made menacingly towards Oscar.

He caught up with him on the edge of our penalty area so Yours Truly had a grandstand view of Muffitt's Last Stand. It was Judgement Day for Oscar, and he knew it, but to his credit, he stood his ground and even stuck out a square defiant chin.

"Come 'ere, yer cheatin' bastard," muttered Keith, and he landed a mighty, meaty fist on Oscar's jaw. The resounding slap of the bone-crunching smack echoed around the trees, along the canal bank and down the players' tunnel of the last forty years. "Let's see yer bawlin' now," were Keith's words of farewell to the Yorkshire Old Boys' League. He refused to pay his fine, feeling it to be entirely unjustified and, to this day, the League records still contain the infamous entry:

MUFFITT K.   Old Batelians   banned - *sine die*

One of the most endearing features of the Old Boys' League was the wit and repartee of many of its combatants. You had to keep your head well down in any changing-room before or after a match if you wanted to

" ...Let's see yer bawlin' now."

avoid becoming the butt of a clever remark. Such playful banter was generally referred to as "piss-taking", and your ability to ride it out marked you down as either "one of the lads" or as "a funny bugger". If you happened to fall into the latter category, then your footballing career was probably best completed elsewhere...

From the age of twenty-four or so, I suddenly began to notice that more and more of the senior players amongst my playing colleagues had to administer fairly extensive health-care before taking the field. A variety of devices was employed in this pursuit, and my teacher-statistician's eye very quickly observed that the amount of time spent in such activity was directly proportional to the age of the players involved.

I changed and played with 60 year old Victor Steel [Old Batelians] and with Brian Hirst [Wheelwright Old Boys] who managed regular Third Team appearances long after receiving his statutory OAP bus-pass. Such players would arrive in the changing-room shortly before one o'clock for a three o'clock kick-off, open a suitcase brimming with medical supplies and set about doctoring their ageing bodies.

Thereafter, there was a steady stream of players arriving at set intervals: forty-five year olds at 1.45pm; forty year olds at 2pm; thirty year olds at 2.15pm. Each set brought their own suitcases of medical supplies so by the time the youngsters arrived - any time between 2.40pm and 2.59pm - the changing-room resembled a First Aid Station on the Western Front.

There were bandages, bottles of liniment, trusses, syringes, plaster casts, stethoscopes and surgical tongs littering the floors of all the changing-rooms I frequented, all the said paraphernalia being put to individual use to ensure survival over the coming ninety minutes. And as such activity progressed, I noticed how the individual shapes of the players changed quite dramatically.

A mere strip of a forty year old, thin and wiry in his approaching old age, would suddenly assume the proportions of an Olympic weight-lifter,such was the amount of padding and protection he wore about his bodily parts. If you hadn't been present to witness the change taking place, you would have played the subsequent game from the first whistle quaking in abject fear of such giants. In any event, it was a source of unceasing wonder to ponder the fact that such old men must have been as fit as proverbial lops to lug around all that extra weight for the statutory ninety minute period. It was also the source of much changing-room banter:

"Oh, Croftie! Won't yer feet fall off wi' t'weight of all that bandage round thi' ankles?"

"What's t'wife usin' ter keep up 'er stockings today then, Ken?"

"Sithee! Ah see Fred's gorr 'is mother's corset on again."

" 'Ave yer any room left fer yer tacklin' in all that wrappin', Victor?"

"Ey up, Mossie! Tha's got thi legs on upside down."

Banter was the main feature of play throughout the Old Boys League. I've known a game actually come to a temporary halt as a result of the helpless laughter of all participants, including the referee. A chance remark or a witty quip during the actual conduct of a game was a skill which I lacked but I've always envied those who possess it. And none more so than Brian Roberts [Wheelwright Old Boys] to whom we referred as "The Laird of Saviletown".

Brian, a stocky, blond-haired well-educated intellectual, was adept at shielding the ball from opponents by turning his back and awaiting support from his own players. Often, he would hold the ball for an eternity whilst anticipating the expected cavalry charge up-field. Often, he was disappointed. Often, he was unceremoniously kicked from behind as a result. On such ocasions, whilst fending off the physical attentions of a craggy, stubble-chinned centre-half, the Laird would issue a velvet, educated, indignant appeal over his erudite shoulder to the Man-in-Black:

"I say, referee! Does this chap know *who* I am???" or "Goodness me, referee! Are we all playing the same game?" On the rare award of a free-kick against him: "Well, heavens above, referee - I felt that decision was a trifle harsh..."

But the Laird reached his peak of genteel wit at the beginning of one game before we had even put serious boot to ball. We'd gone a goalkeeper short at the eleventh hour, so a Fourth Team stand-by had been drafted in to plug the gap. A rotund lump of lard with a huge beer-drinker's gut extending to the edge of the six-yard box, Fatso only succeeded in being selected when the Fourth team were short. But today, he was Our Hero - dragged out of bed in dire circumstances at 2.00pm to fill the breach.

The Laird left the changing-rooms in fine style and trotted into our penalty area for a spot of kicking-in before the match proper. As he drew within earshot, he came up with his carefully considered banter, loud enough for all to hear but addressed directly to Frank Goodall [Captain]: "I say, Skipper, I had no idea our 'keeper was pregnant. Do you think he ought to play in that condition?"

Amateur football of this kind is a lesson for life - how to cope with the taunts and jibes of team-mates, with the two imposters Triumph and Disaster and with facing up to the Awful Truth of the Passing Years. And such a truth hit me square between the eyes one dismal, wet Saturday afternoon in February 1978...

The rain is lashing on the teeth of a howling gale as I proudly lead out Wheelwright Old Boys' Thirds for an encounter with St Bede's Old Boys, somewhere on a council estate in deepest Bradford.

At the age of thirty-four, I now regard each game played to a finish as a bite of the Forbidden Fruit - as sweet as the nectar of the Gods. Every completed ninety minutes of frolicking fun has been pinched from beneath the very nose of the dreaded "Anno Domini" which is creeping on apace. My knees have stiffened, my ankles are giving way, my back is crooked, and I have become the sad possessor of a medical supplies suitcase. Hitching up my corset-like jock-strap with its whale-bone extension, I trot proudly and defiantly to the centre circle to toss up.

Our game progresses and in defence, we are confronted by an opposing forward line containing several dashing young blades who, truth to tell, were no great shakes as footballers if St Bede's Thirds was the best they could manage. We have to chase them round for most of the first half but we manage to hold out and we even mount some attacks on their goal, thus allowing time for Rest and Recuperation in our back line. However, for Yours Truly, the game is marked by one strange feature.

Every time their winger receives a pass, the young blade at centre-forward shouts: "Shove it past, Baldy!" or "Knock it over, Baldy". Believing Baldy to be the nickname for a member of their forward line, I strived to anticipate their next move as soon as I heard that name called. Indeed, I was successful in preventing several of their attacks bearing fruit as a result. The exact identity of this particular player remained a mystery right up to the half-time whistle when the scores remained level and we gathered round in the rain and wind for the customary five minutes' break.

I look round "the lads" and contemplate the prospect of a second-half against the wind. Steam rises from our sweating flanks; our faces and shirts are soaked and streaked with black mud; our hair has been flattened to our scalps by the incessant rain. All in all, we look a poor, bedraggled lot to be facing another forty-five testing minutes. But shaking off my doubts about our staying power, I make an earnest attempt to infuse enthusiasm into the team with a stirring captain's address,

We trudge to our positions for the second half, and almost as an afterthought, I put the question which has been puzzling me throughout the first period of play: "Hey, fellers! Which one is 'Baldy'? Who are they talking about?"

Almost to a man, our Wheelwright team collapses in guffaws of stifled laughter. Some of them begin hooting and holding their sides in helpless mirth whilst I remain puzzled.

"Dun't tha know?" asks Alan Austerfield, playing today in the Ray Wilson style of overlapping full-back. "Well, just thee look in t'mirror when we've done. Tha'll know then."

The game ended in a most satisfactory 0-0 draw and I made straight for the dressing-room mirror. Wiping away the steamy mist, I saw a mud-streaked old man with harrowed furrows round his eyes and a hang-dog look on his ageing face. But above all, winking mockingly at me through matted hair, I could just make out the tell-tale pink skin of denuded scalp and the awful truth slowly dawned: "Who's Baldy?? It was ME!!!"

My footballing career came to a swift end after that. I was never the same player again. The prospect of joining the ranks of wrinkly "ancients" knocked the stuffing out of me and I sadly hung up my boots along with my medical supplies case. Instead, I turned reluctantly to spending Saturday afternoons cultivating leeks and other wholesome vegetables on my own allotment.

But it'll never match that wholesome thrill of charging about a football field half-dressed, in the company of your mates; going through the back door of the town-centre Little Saddle half an hour before opening time for post-match refreshment; re-living and recounting each glorious minute of that afternoon's game; re-telling the legendary tales of yester-year; selecting the teams and eagerly relishing the prospect of next week's encounter...

And even now, at the age when many of my generation have become grandads, I still feel the special atmosphere of Saturday afternoons. As the church clock strikes three, I look away from my neat rows of Saturday afternoon cabbages and leeks and gaze longingly into the dim and distant seasons of yesterday.

I can still head a good ball and talk a good game, can't I?

I could still run around on the wing, couldn't I? But the awful truth is that my body refuses to join in with such emotional aspirations...

Shouts from the nearby football field interrupt my rêverie. Was that a call of encouragement or a desperate plea to the Man-in-Black? Or was it a distant echo from those glorious pitches of long ago, gently whispered in the wind-rustle of the leaves on the nearby trees:

"Ey up, Mossie! Tha's got thi legs on upside down..."

***

"THEY HAVEN'T A SHOP..."

Half-a-dozen years after that KOYLI learning experience at Magilligan Point, it was *my* turn to be in charge. Following an exhaustingly difficult route-march through A-levels, and a pleasant stroll through Teacher Training at Goldsmiths' College, London, I emerged in the summer of 1966 clutching a Teacher's Certificate. This was my authentic qualification to become a Leader of Men [or rather small boys between the ages of 11 and 16] back home in the Old Country.

I returned "up North" to my Shoddy Town haunts - the place where I felt I *really* belonged - and began the search for a job. In those days, they grew on trees. Help yourself to the one you fancied, and if it doesn't work out, well, there's plenty more where that one came from...

George Christopher Locke, Headmaster of Batley Boys' High School, ushered me like a mother hen and her only chick into his office. I almost gasped aloud at the impressive panoramic view from his office window. Overlooking a summer-holiday deserted playing field, the green slopes tumbled away dramatically to the rooftop rows and mill-chimneys of 1960's industrial Batley. Taylor's Mill stack still cast its gloomy shadow over the soot-stained terraces below, as it had for as long as I could remember, and I was tempted to stroll across to the picture-window to seek out other landmarks.

But this was no time for sight-seeing, as the tall, bald George Christopher launched enthusiastically into his welcome to me as a newly appointed teacher of French, English, Games [and anything else going at the time].

"Now believe me, those boys will be a picture when they turn up for school next week," he mused fondly. "Oh yes - in their new blazers, new school ties and their smart satchels - they'll be a picture."

There was no doubting Our Revered Leader's enthusiasm.

He believed, as many in that generation did, that "education" meant something more than book-learning and Maths and passing exams which dominated the educational diet on offer just across the road, at the Grammar School. The bed-rock of his Headmaster's philosophy was that lads from the back streets of Batley should all travel to the far reaches of the Yorkshire Dales to experience life "in the raw".

For the general population of 1960's Batley, this was like talking in the accents of a wild-eyed Dervish from Katmandu such was the likelihood of being understood. In Batley, we were only just beginning to incorporate into our daily thinking the fact that we'd won World War Two, so the idea that groups of boys should hare up and down the slopes of Ingleborough, Whernside or Pen-y-Ghent had all the credibility of setting off for the Moon on scooters [or bubble-cars].

However, it's 1966, shortly after Bobby Moore and his men have done their World Cup bit for English pride, and I've been successfully appointed to the George Christopher Locke Crusade. I was ready for the fray.

Fresh from my college training, bright-eyed and bushy-tailed, I was keen and eager to contribute to an educational dream back home in the Heavy Woollen District, amongst those dark, satanic mills which had dominated my youthful existence. Our Revered Leader must have been thinking along the same lines, because I can't help pondering that my success in landing my first teaching post had been due, in no mean part, to the fact that my application form included the words "Duke of Edinburgh's Award - Gold Standard".

George C. had seized on this, and in a cursory job-interview lasting all of five minutes I was appraised of his educational love: Outdoor Pursuits and The Batley High School for Boys Activity Centre. [for ease of reference - "The Hut"]

There it stood, in a field just over the bridge through Little Stainforth, on the right hand side of the track - the edifice which was one of the main features of my early teaching life. It was, in fact, an old cricket pavilion with a verandah and a tea-room, but to Batley lads of the 1960's, it was home for several spells during their years at the High School.

Fitted out with bunks and a kitchen, and standing only two hundred yards from the river and Stainforth Force where we swam and rigged up a "death-slide", it was an idyllic spot to spend the week-end. But *not* with twenty or so 12 and 13 year-old adolescents from Woodsome Estate, Carlinghow and Healey. Some of these lads had never left home in their lives before but, doggedly following the dictats of George Christopher's philosophy, time spent at the Activities Centre, in the company of their Form Teacher, would be an important part of their *total* education.

So it was then, that with a deepening sense of foreboding and all of nine months' classroom experience under my belt, I was driven up to Stainforth in the school bus [another of George Christopher's innovations] on a Friday evening in June to spend an educational week-end with the lads in my form. Bernard Schofield [Metalwork] drove the bus up the winding North Yorkshire lanes past sleepy farm yards and dozing cattle in rolling, late-afternoon fields, through Gargrave, Hellifield, Long Preston and on to Little Stainforth.

A feeling of utter gloom and despondency weighed down on my erstwhile youthfully enthusiastic shoulders.

"What am I doing here," I moaned to myself amidst the monkey-chatter aboard the old Leyland bus. I'd had to forego a 2nd XI cricket match at home; I was going to be "mum" to twenty lads [some of whom were quite naughty at school]; I was in charge all on my own. By the time the bus chugged to a halt in the lane below the Hut, I had settled into a heavy depression, re-inforced by the gathering twilight and the approach of bed-time.

However, according to the gospel of George C., there was a set routine for daily life at the Hut. It was all typed up

102

on duplicated sheets, and its pre-conceived plan just *had* to be followed to the letter, on pain of severe admonishment in the office upon return to school.

There was a published agenda for everything: Bed-time Arrangements, Catering Policy, Ablutions Rota and a Physical Activities Schedule. Every waking minute of every waking day was boldly franked "GCL", so we teachers had to see that our young charges stuck to it. The idle sods amongst us couldn't palm off all the foul tasks onto the lads and sit with our feet up - we had to join in or suffer starvation and full latrine buckets...

The old bus disappeared down the lane in a cloud of blue diesel smoke and chugged out of sight as I waved Bernard a fond, goodbye. Up the path, my line of twenty little chicks with their suitcases and rucksacks waited reverently at the foot of the verandah steps.

What was I to do for the next 72 hours with twenty Batley lads who were scheduled to experience the joys of life in the Dales? [Roll on Sunday at 4.00pm when the school bus would chug up to the entrance of the track and we'd head for home.]

The inevitable request: "Sir, can we go swimmin' ?"

A hasty read-through of George C.'s schedule indicated that the first evening was to be spent on:

1. preparing a meal
2. consuming it
3. kitchen and cleaning duties
4. a game of rounders in the field
5. cocoa and bed.

"We'll save that for tomorrow, Oakland. We've got something far more exciting for this evening, lad..."

Oh, how the time dragged! Thank goodness smoking wasn't the taboo it is now - at least I could enjoy a pleasant Woodbine, sitting on the verandah in the late evening sunshine, supervising rounders from a safe distance. Several of the lads were probably round the back

103

of the Hut having a sly swaller" themselves, but I must admit, I wasn't going out of my way to catch them. That would have meant my giving them the slipper, thus spoiling the atmosphere of teamwork and enjoyment. And the highlight of the week-end was yet to come: tomorrow's walk over Smearsett Scar looming behind us - on to Austwick via the hamlet of Feizor - and back! But this required a good night's sleep in preparation for its arduous demands...

After the ten o'clock cup of cocoa and the scheduled twenty minute ritual of pre-bedtime washing, teeth-cleaning and weeing, it was time for the lads to retire.

I remember that this was achieved without a great deal of fuss but then there came the embarrassing moment when Sir was due to retire himself - and this meant getting into night attire watched by twenty pairs of ridiculing adolescent eyes. The teachers were not given separate rooms so we slept in a bunk in the same room as the lads.

A horrifying thought now struck me - I was going to have to drop my drawers, bare my nethers and climb into my "'jamas" in front of these lads.

There were stifled snorts and titters from beneath blankets as I contrived to hide my important bits and when my bare bum accidentally peeped out for some evening air, there was a guffaw from the other side of the dormitory.

Oh joy! All this, and I would have to face the same lads in a Monday morning classroom.

"Good night, boys" I said imperiously as I climbed into the top bunk near the door. "Lights out!"

"Good night, sir" some chorused as I leaned out of the bunk and switched off the lights.

After a few brief moments of silent rustling and adjusting to the uncomfortable bunks, a small adolescent voice rang crystal-clear through the absolute darkness:

"Good night, Fred!"

Peals of boyish laughter and hoots of dare-devil glee.

Lights on. I leapt out of bed and bellowed "Oakland! Come 'ere!!"

Oakland it was who had decided to have some fun and had dared to call me by my first name. I grabbed the nearest slipper and ordered the traditional bum-up position. The slipper descended with a mighty crack, Oakland yelped obligingly, and the lads were as well behaved all week-end as girls in a convent.

The following morning, after the GCL-prescribed breakfast of bacon and beans, there came the preparation of sandwiches. Now, for many of the lads from homes where the staple diet was usually taken from a newspaper in front of the telly, preparing a lunch-time sandwich was a mind-blowingly new experience. As you might expect, the process was itemised step-by-George-Christopher-Locke-step on a duplicated sheet.

The filling for the bleached white bread slices was a sickly, pale yellow "Sandwich Spread". Each dollop of the mixture remindedus of Sunday morning piles in the road left by Saturday evening revellers back home after a "reight good neet on t'ale". This impression was reinforced by the appearance of bright orange pieces of diced carrot winking at us from the yellow slime as we daubed it on our daily bread.

Many of the catering crew made extremely accurate honking noises as they glued the chunky yellow paste into place. As a result, one or two of the boys with a weaker constitution paled significantly and began wretching uncontrollably.

They had to dash outside and part company with their recent GCL breakfasts so, for a while, it became very difficult indeed to differentiate between the genuine Sandwich Spread and the Human Product, both containing as they did, a preponderance of diced carrot.

However, after wrapping, counting and allocating the completed sandwiches, filling water-bottles and collecting ruck-sacks, the group was eventually ready for a full day's experience of walking in the Dales. The start had been successfully delayed as long as possible to allow the pewkers among the sandwich-makers time to recover, and the itinerary for the day had been kept intentionally simple. After all, they were only 12 and 13 year olds, so at around 11.30am, we toiled up the track beside the Hut in the hot sunshine of the approaching noon.

Thirty minutes passed and we entered the sleepy hamlet of Feizor, whereupon the search for "t'shop" began.

In thirty years of taking various groups out walking in the countryside, it has never failed to amaze me that "townies" from Batley and Dewsbury regard any collection of rustic dwellings randomly encountered along the leafy lanes of England's green and pleasant land as the automatic location of a corner-shop. This therefore represents the opportunity to spend hard-earned pocket-money on trash confectionery. And these boys were no exception.

They scoured the sleepy Dales hamlet for fully ten minutes with all the thoroughness of those nasty Nazi patrols in old war films, before returning breathlessly after a fruitless search.

They gasped in astonished incredulity: "Sir, they haven't a shop!"

Hard-earned "spend" was returned to their pockets and, for all of them, this was the week-end's most amazing and consequently world-shattering discovery - a village "baht a shop...!"

Undaunted, we trecked on, efficiently guided by OS Map Sheet 196, up tracks and paths, past farm yards with dogs and cattle and horses. Vividly recalled by most of the Monday-morning class upon their return to civilisation, we discovered, by the side of a track near Dead Man's Cave, next to a wall, rotting in the afternoon sun and festooned in buzzing blue-bottles, the remains of a dead sheep. This gave rise to further constitutional crises amongst the pewkers in the Sandwich Preparation Group, but eventually, undaunted, we made our intrepid way to Scar Close Farm and the ascent of Smearsett Scar....

"We're not goin' up there, are we sir? It's a mountain!"

"Of course we are, Kirk," I replied, sneaking a glance at my watch and calculating that we'd manage this little test and arrive back at the Hut at 4 o'clock to begin preparation of the evening meal. "It's nobbut a pimple, is this."

"But, sir, we've walked miles. Can't we catch t'bus 'ome now?"

"Not likely, lad. They don't have buses out 'ere, and anyway, this is what life in the Dales is all about - *fresh air, long walks* and *succulent sarnies.* Come on, then! Last to the top's a custard!"

After the intial race over walls and a couple of meadows, the pace slowed to a dogged plod, but we make it eventually, and the view from the top, overlooking Feizor Wood and Austwick was appreciated by all.

After a relieved descent, it wasn't long before we were all sitting on the roadside of the village, hungrily wolfing our succulent sandwiches. The mid-day repast lasted all of ten minutes whereupon, one of the pewkers whose complexion had maintained its sickly pallor all morning asked if he might "recce" the area for a shop.

Permission granted, he made a miraculous return to full fitness. Leaping to his feet, he whizzed off into the distance, eagerly brandishing a pound note and shouting to his chums: "Ey up! Sir sez Ah can go an' look fer a shop..."

In the twinkling of an eye, he was back, laden with bars of chocolate, packets of crisps, Black Sambo's and small bottles of pop. "Ey.... this is a *reight* place is this, Sir!" he chortled between great gobfuls of chocolate and flavoured crisps. "They've a reight good shop, 'ere. Not like over yonder..." and he jerked a fully- recovered, derisory nod in the direction of Feizor...

We'd covered about 8 miles on our treck, and when we finally arrived back at the Hut at about 4pm as planned, you'd have thought the lads were returning from an expedition to the Himalayas, such was their relief to be "home".

Rucksacks were flung gratefully on bunks; boots were-dragged gruntingly from tired feet; aching bodies were stretched somnolently on the grass below the verandah. The peace of utter exhaustion filtered gently down through the late-afternoon sunshine and settled on the Activities Centre. Just for a few brief moments, the tranquil gurgling sound of brown Dales water over Stainforth Force whispered up the slope and washed over our aching bodies...

And so began a succession of visits to The Hut which were a cornerstone of my early career at Batley High School for Boys. I soon became a seasoned veteran as I accompanied lads of all shapes and sizes in all kinds of weather. Often we would curse the Dales downpours and treacherous mists, or herald the arrival of summer as we frolicked about in the cooling waters of Stainforth Force. Amongst it all, I don't think that I ever *really* understood the George Christopher doctrine of my early teaching years, but I do know that generations of Batley lads the world over recall with pleasure and delight their time spent "up at t'Hut".

My abiding memory concerns the time when a group of 16 year old Duke of Edinburgh Award trainees went up Pen-y-Ghent in a practice exercise as preparation for their "proper" expedition later in the school year. This particular motley crew were under my supervision for the practice exercise, before tackling the real thing, unaccompanied.

I'd stepped in at the last minute one May weekend because some older and much wiser member of staff had given late back-word. He'd either forgotten to mention the missing week-end to "'Er Indoors" or he'd read the long range weather forecast.

In any event, I'd been press-ganged to fill the breach by George Christopher, to whom a "tin-horn" recruit dared not say "No, I'm very sorry, Mr Locke, but I've been selected to play for Liversedge 2nd XI and I am a key member of the side..." [most of which would have been a lie in any case]. So there I was, a late recruit to the "Leader of Men" group.We arrived in Little Stainforth under ominous Friday afternoon skies, based at the Hut for the week-end to practise our map-and-compass skills and to spend a couple of nights under canvas.

The ritual of settling in was performed swiftly and efficiently following the GCL schedule - these lads had had five years at it - and I was beginning to anticipate a pleasant and restful night inside, in any of the bunks of my choice.

The trainees would be spending a night under canvas and preparing their own evening meal, so the whole enterprise was beginning to assume the proportions of the proverbial "bobby's job" as I supervised tent pitching in the field below the Hut. All had gone smoothly from my young teacher's point of view and the lads settled down for a restful night's slumber beneath the starlit Dales sky...

But the eerie silence of the rustic night was soon ripped apart by violent thunder cracks, sizzling bolts of lightning and successive torrential downpours. The wind howled around the eaves of the Hut and at 2am, seven drowned rats crawled in from the weather, soaked and shivering, to sleep in the relative comfort of the bunk-beds.

The tents were abandoned to the ravages of the wild winds while we drifted off into fitful slumber through the rain-on-roof thrash of yet another downpour. There wasn't one of us who relished the prospect of tomorrow's carefully-prepared exercise trek up Pen-y-Ghent.

An early morning peep from the window revealed four tents billowing like tea-clipper sails in the wind, heaving and straining at their aluminium poles, but still intact. We donned our water-proof capes before breakfast and lugged them into the dining area to dry out.

Relishing every last morsel of our GCL-prescribed bacon-and-beans, we attempted to predict our immediate future. You see, this was 1967. Nobody carried the modern-day, obligatory ghetto-blaster/walkman/mobile phone and we hadn't even so much as a small "trannie" with which to access the airwaves for a desperately needed weather forecast. So between mouthfuls of succulent bacon, anxious eyes gazed up at the skies for signs of improvement.

And how the fickle Dales weather strung us along!

By ten o'clock, the wind had dropped, the clouds had rolled away and the sun shone brightly through. Full of optimism and a renewed zest for life, we stepped out on our trek, through Little Stainforth, along Goat Lane towards Halton Gill and the brave ascent of Pen-y-Ghent.

Now I have to say that up to this point, the map-and-compass exercise had been achieved in efficient and exemplary fashion according to our GCL Gospel. Amongst those Shoddy Town lads, sitting on the very crest of Pen-y-Ghent, enjoying the exhilarating views of Whernside and Ingleborough, there was an air of smug achievement.

We lay back on our rucksacks, gazed into an azure sky and sighed a sigh of ecstatic contentment...

And then that perfidious Dales weather struck again!

In the twinkling of an eye, the clouds rolled up, the sky darkened, the wind blustered and blew menacingly, and the rain began to teem. The spectacular views vanished as thickening purple and black clouds descended, blanket-like, around us. The distant Whernside was snatched away; Ingleborough disappeared; and before we knew it, we were negotiating our descent in an envelope of dense, grey Dales fog.

Panic was but a veneer slice away from our conscious thoughts as we picked our uncertain ways through clumps of thick bracken. Echoes of other errant expeditions began to surface in my mind as the lads began their fearful mutterings to each other through the dense, foggy cloud:

"Yer useless pillock - tha couldn't read a map if thi life depended on it..."

"We're bloody lost nar. What are we gunner do?? Wes'll never ger 'ome now."

But fear not! Lacking a Rastus Copsey on this occasion,we were saved by the GCL Gospel, which is abundantly clear on emergency tactics in such life-threatening circumstances.

All my training manuals had described the painstaking and laborious method of sending a group-member out in front with white handkerchief whilst compass-bearings were taken at the limit of visibility, ensuring the safety of all group members at all times. But I'd never actually *had* to do it - in real life, and in charge, and fully responsible for the safety of my pupils. Besides which, I was looking after *me*, and as far as I was concerned, what happened to me was important. So we set off, employing the pre-scribed method.

After carefully calculating compass-bearings from our sodden OS Sheet 196 map, I despatched one of the lads in the direction of "down" with a handkerchief. Waving it frantically and shouting all the while, he proceeds gingerly across the heather until he is *almost* swallowed up in the the thick grey swirl.

At this point, we scream at him to stand still and rush down to join him, whereupon the whole process is repeated.

After about and hour or so of such deliberate and tedious orienteering, the rain is beginning to seep through to skin-depth, the cloud is thickening ever faster and frozen feet are squelching in leaden, sodden footwear. And then, the magic moment arrives...

It's 1967. I'm 23 years old and I'm in charge of a group of 16 year olds, half-way down [perhaps?] one of the famous Three Peaks. We're all soaked to the skin, wishing we were back home, on Commercial Street, Mayman Lane, Woodsome Estate - anywhere in dear old Batley will do.

We've covered about six hundred yards of our descent "blind" - on compass bearings only - in pouring, drench-ing rain and ever-descending, thickening cloud. Six

Shoddy Town lads and their teacher, cowering and crouching in the shelter of a low wall. We're taking stock of the situation and I am desperately re-folding my papier-mâché map in yet another attempt to locate our position.

I glance round the group.

What a miserable, wet-through, hang-dog-looking bunch!

Water drips down and off the end of every miserable, down-cast Shoddy Town nose. Huddled under their waterproof capes, the group remind me of those faded, yellowing photographs of Life on the Somme, 1916. Not a smile or a cheery word from anyone.

Palmer looks imploringly at me. "Sir, is it awreyt if we 'ave a smoke?"

Now, what you have to understand is that in those far-off days, a Teacher was an important member of society's Army of Proper People. Along with Vicars, Policemen and Mums and Dads, Teachers were responsible for the moral up-bringing of young folk - the righteous-living and honest adults of the future generation. And here I am, a Teacher, responsible "*in loco parentis*" for these boys.

I care for them as if they were my only little chicks as I try desperately to instill in them the virtues of a healthy outdoor life and the manly values of the Duke of Edinburgh's Award Scheme. I administer the discipline which comes with close-knit teamwork and caring for your fellow-human-beings.

I'm an Important Figure in these lads' lives - and Palmer's asking me if they can *SMOKE*???

"Aye, lad, why not? I'm fair gasping for one... Have you a light with you?" was my heartfelt, Dales-drenched reply as I delved beneath my waterproof for my packet of Woodbines.

***

"Sir, is it awreyt if we 'ave a smoke?"

DWYGYFYLCHI PIE

I woke, startled stiff in the thick blackness of the two-man ridge tent. The nagging stab of a full bladder had burst into my dreams and I sat bolt upright in the wooden-framed camp-bed clutching my lower abdomen.

The stinking tent-latrines were at least sixty yards down the field towards the silently sleeping seaside town of Penmaenmawr. For instant relief, I would have to dress appropriately to fend off the cold chill of the night air and make my way across No Man's Land. All such activity would undoubtedly rouse George Christopher from his Headmaster's peaceful slumber in the camp-bed opposite me, so I decided to give it a miss until morning.

I turned over, mentally switched off the ringing tones from my bladder, and fell to contemplating my lot in an attempt to return to somnolence...

This was my first experience of yet another facet of George Christopher Locke's life-long educational mission - Annual School Camp.

Our Revered Leader [ORL] at Batley Boy's High School was utterly convinced that he was at the forefront of educational thinking. Sticking doggedly to his personal philosophy, he issued regular edicts about Outdoor Pursuits. All Shoddy Town lads who came under his care were in dire need of escape from the looming shadows of those dark satanic mills, and in order to effect this, the bulk of the school population would migrate *en masse* across the country to experience a fortnight under canvas. Thus, our entire summer term revolved around ORL's intricately planned exodus of lads from the back streets of Batley to rural North Wales.

We teachers all willingly fell in with such an avid sense of vocation. It allowed us to escape the daily drudgery of the classroom struggle to control thirty or so raw-boned, red-faced, reluctant Shoddy Town lads, and it presented us with salaried licence to roam free in the Great Outdoors.

Along with our professional colleagues, we took responsibility for the round-the-clock welfare of perhaps 80 - 100 boys away from "home". *We* supervised their Outdoor Pursuits activities while the rest of the school continued with a skeleton staff and the "rag ends" of boys who failed to attend Camp.

Now, on this particular occasion, the Old Hands on the BHS staff - seasoned campaigners at this Summer Camp lark - chortled with glee as they allocated my kipping-quarters sharing a tent with ORL. It wasn't exactly a bundle of laughs.

As Headmaster of a large secondary school, George Christopher had maintained a professional "distance" from Yours Truly - a young and inexperienced new boy on the staff. In the normal course of a working week, hardly a word was exchanged between us as he swept along corridors and into offices on his daily rounds of the school. But now, in a field above this Welsh seaside town, it was my nightly joy to bare my nethers in front of my Boss as I scrambled into pyjamas with a respectful and polite "Goodnight, Mr Locke".

It was a price I had to pay as a new recruit to the teaching profession. And at least it was better than ploughing through a pile of green exercise books every night until the small hours, marking and assessing the inane scrawlings of thirteen year old Shoddy Town adolescents.

An air of rural tranquility washed over me as I contemplated my lot in the silent peace of the dark night. This was the first time I had ever been to North Wales and met with its sleepy tranquility and quaint "foreign" places - Llanystumtdwy, Afon Wen, Dwygyfylchi, Llanfairfechan - *and* I was being paid for the privilege!

Yes, it wasn't a bad life being a young teacher in 1967, I inwardly mused, drifting gently back into the land of Nod...

Perhaps an hour later, I sat bolt upright in my camp-bed

once again, but this time, convinced that some alien invader was inserting his light-sabre up my external urinary part and thrusting it deep into the inner recesses of my lower abdomen. The contents of my distended bladder seemed ready to flood forth in a torrential burst of monsoon-like properties; I *had* to make those tent-latrines - *and quick*! In a forlorn attempt to avoid dousing the sleeping Headmaster in a fount of warm spent fluid, I desperately clutched my nethers in one hand and prepared to abandon ship. Forsaking all consideration for ORL's peaceful slumber, I shot out of bed into the dark, yanked on my walking boots, pulled a track-suit top round my shoulders and made a desperately hasty but silent exit into the North Wales moonlight.

Running the length of the field to reach the latrines had ceased to be an option about an hour ago, such was the leaden sag of my bladder. Supporting the full organ with both hands cupped underneath, I began to shamble my way down the field like a pyjama-clad OAP in a sack-race - placing one painstaking foot in front of another, taking one slow, cumbersome step at a time.

Half way down the field, I considered instant relief there and then, feeling certain that I wasn't going to make the privacy of the musty-smelling, hessian-shrouded latrine tents, but I quickly abandoned the idea. The Niagara Falls gush of falling pee would undoubtedly wake the entire camp, so I tip-toed on for what seemed an age.

I shuffled agonisingly past the boys' tents and the kitchen tent and on beyond the dining-room marquee. Racked by searing stabs in my bladder, I inched my way out into the open tracts of No Man's Land towards the latrines which Health and Safety considerations dictated to be a secure and sanitary distance from the dining area.

Bent double to support the liquid weight, I felt as if I was holding up a steel vat full of urine between my legs, and my leaden progress came to a shambling halt. Half-way across the still and silent tract of land, I could shuffle no more and, in a desperate fury of frantic fumbling in the pale moonlight, I located my drain-tap and let the lot go in the middle of the Unoccupied Zone.

The pent up torrent of hot wee hit the North Wales terrain at the lightning speed which only comes with desperate relief, and an ecstatic smile of pure joy lit my erstwhile contorted face. The sound of the torrent echoed round the sombre shapes of the No Man's Land trees waking two or three sleeping owls, but I cared not a jot, such was the easing of my discomfort.

After what seemed like fully five minutes of bladder relaxation [and my parting company with *gallons* of spent fluid], the awful realisation now dawned. Such a roaring deluge of human water must surely have woken our entire contingent of sleeping Batley lads. At this very minute, they would be peering under their fly-sheets into the moonlit expanse of No Man's Land, splitting their collective sides at Sir having to relieve himself during the night.

In as dignified a manner as possible, I adjusted my nocturnal attire and turned to make my long embarrassed way back to my tent.

In my mind's eye, I could vividly picture at this very moment, ORL preparing a speech of admonishment for his newly appointed member of staff, doubtless considering my dismissal from the staff of the school. I was ready for the worst, but to my utter amazement, there was no sound to disturb the night air amongst any of the tents past which I crept. No sound, that is, save for one - a tent occupied by Fourth Year lads who knew their camp ropes from three previous George Christopher Crusades.

As I sneaked warily past guy-ropes and fly-sheets, I caught the sound of adolescent awakenings - a gutteral rumbling accompanied by a muffled snort or two. And then the words: "Ey up, Jacko! Did y'ear that???

"What y'on abaht?"

"Must be pissin' it darn artside. That means wes'll get wet tomorrer..."

117

The following crisp and clear, sunlit morning duly arrived and I made my sheepish way to the marquee for the first meal of the new day. Expecting jibes and clever remarks about my nocturnal mishap from my colleagues and derisory behind-the-hand laughs from the lads, I put on a brave face and whistled my way along the aisles of wooden trestle tables.

To my relieved surprise, there were no snide remarks and no derisory smirks. With the heartfelt joy of having got away with my nocturnal toilet activities, I sat down to tackle my stipulated George Christopher Camp Breakfast...

The Camp Menu according to ORL was indeed A Many Splendoured Thing. Planned in his Headmaster's Office with great relish throughout the dark days of winter, the regular weekly Camp Diet Sheet was so devised that it caused the fewest possible technical problems for amateur caterers. It thus consisted of wonderfully contrived and invented menus, designed to fill the Heavy Woollen bellies of Batley lads by kidding their alimentary canals that they were stuffed full to bursting.

This served to send each camp member home with the impression that he'd been admirably fed and watered for the entire period of his rural stay. Moreover, it guaranteed that he'd be one of the first to put his name down for next year's camp when the Autumn volunteering time came round again!

So those menus all included vast quantities of bulk-inducing ingredients. Sausages from the local butcher ram-jam full of oatmeal; regular daily intakes of dried [powdered] egg; thick, creamy sandwich spread, dried mashed potato-concentrate. And *custard*. Gallons and gallons of thick, sweet, creamy-rich *custard*.

Not only did the carefully prescribed menus include precise information on quantities of ingredients to be taken out of the Store Tent, but they also included instructions on cooking methods to make the dietary offer a little more exciting. Most of the cooking was done on portable gas burners, but there were some Camp Ovens to enable the more adventurous of the daily Kitchen Duty Groups to attempt exotic, culinary effects for our communal delight.

And so it came to pass that, at this point in my teaching career, I savoured the delights of Dwygyfylchi Pie...

We named this particular dish by careful reference to our Ordnance Survey Map Sheet Number 115 where we found, close by the seaside town of Penmaenmawr, a pub in the village of that strangely spelt name. The nectar on tap at the pub, however, paled into insignificance alongside the food of the Gods that was this particular George Christopher Culinary Creation.

It was, in fact, a rhubarb crumble made with fairly ordinary ingredients and cooked in the antiquated, rickety gas ovens of the standing camp kitchen. What made it addictively desirable was the addition of bag upon bag of sugar to negate the sourness of the tinned rhubarb [WRCC Catering Department issue]. The final product was even sweeter than the sickly condensed milk of light-weight ration fame. But of course, every good Shoddy Town school kid of the 60's knows that no rhubarb pie is complete without its topping of rich, golden custard.

Now, the standard Camp Custard to accompany this Pie of Pies was also a George Locke creation and, just like the recipe for the pie, it, too, contained instructions on the addition of a hugely generous amount of flowing white granular sweetness. The hallowed portals of the London Stock Exchange would reverberate resoundingly as the annual word went round that Batley High School Summer camp had started once more and the value of Tate and Lyle shares soared as a result...

Armed with his step-by-step instruction manual on the start-to-finish creation of the dish, each member of staff [assisted by the Kitchen Duty Group of boys] would strain, strive and sweat tears of blood to surpass the succulence of the previous Duty Groups' efforts. At evening meal, your culinary success was judged by the queue for "seconds" along with the sheen of the fat boys' platters as they licked them clean in the effort to extract every last milligram of the golden creamy custard.

I've seen boys attack a plateful of the Pie and Custard as soon as it was slopped onto their plates, devour it in an instant whilst still on the move, the thought of parking their bums on a marquee bench never crossing their minds. Licking their camp platter sparklingly clean, they would dash desperately to the back of the queue to line up for "seconds".

Drooling dreamily, they would shuffle agonisingly slowly as the queue advanced to the serving point, and eagerly hold out their plates, only to be met with a stern doubting enquiry from the teacher on duty:

"Rowden? Rowden? Haven't you had your succulent piece of Dwygyfylchi Pie already?"

"Who me, sir? Nivver, sir... This is mi first time, honest, sir..."

A rapturous smile of ecstatic pleasure would always greet an affirmative nod from Sir. A grief-stricken flood of tears was the response to a refusal, accompanied by a grovelling, begging genuflexion and a conniving plea born of abject desperation:

"Sir, mi mother says I 'ave ter ave it for mi piles - she sez it does 'em good..."

And the fun continued as this particular Summer Camp burrowed its way into the fond recollection of my early teaching career...

I vividly recall accompanying a group of thirteen year olds on a bus trip in our rickety old school bus over Llanberis Pass, navigated and led by the indomitable Derek Sykes [Head of Middle School].

On the way back to camp, Syko spots an ice-cream van and decides to have some fun. Waiting craftily until we are round a bend and out of sight of the hapless ice-cream vendor, Derek instructs Bernard Schofield to stop the bus.

Now, the previous Sunday, and following George C. Locke's Standing Pack Drill for Conduct of School Camps, Derek had led a file of boys and staff along the narrow North Wales lanes to a local chapel for Morning Service. The handful of emotional dewy-eyed pensioners, overcome by rapturous joy at the sight of 100 or so uniformed boys filing into Sunday morning chapel, had donated two crisp, green pound notes "to buy the boys some ice-cream". And now, the unexpected lucre is about to be employed for the purpose for which it was given.

A twinkling, mischievous eye is cast round the bus before Derek announces: "Now, see....ah...Schofield...Schoffer. Come 'ere, lad." The smallest, scruffiest boy on the camp is selected to return round the bend to the ice-cream van.

"Take this money, lad, and go back to that ice-cream man and ask him for .... now let me see .... er .... fifty-six 99ers".

In a Shoddy Town burst of under-nourished enthusiasm, Schoffer hares off out of sight, and the rest of us relish the prospect of the returning goodies.

Five minutes pass, during which time rivers of anticipatory saliva begin to run down the central aisle of the rickety old bus.

"Sir, 'e's coming back," was the shout from the back-seat boys. "Burree ant got nowt...."

A disappointed Syko meets Schofield on the bus step. "Well, Schoffer? What have you say for yourself? Where's our 99ers, lad?"

Schofield the Breathless peers upwards, holds out two crumpled, sweaty pound notes and delivers an earnest, tearful reply: "Sir, Ah asked 'im fer fifty-six 99ers - an' 'e dint say nowt. So Ah asked 'im ageean, an' 'e just said: 'F... off' ".

Fifty-two sad and disappointed Batley lads and four dejected teachers were silent all the way back to camp.

A gloomy shadow settled over the whole camp following the lack of confectionery delight in the afternoon, and

Camp Life was in desperate need of a lift. It fell to Chris Jenkins [another young member of staff] to liven things up for us that night.

With a nagging sense of foreboding, I complied willingly with his cunningly contrived plan...

You see, it was a well-known fact amongst we teachers that once the lads were safely tucked up in their tents for the night, they forgot they were under canvas and naively believed the surrounding walls of their tents to be two feet thick. Trusting the confidentiality of their tent environment, they thought they were unheard by the rest of the camp and they would proceed to conduct conversations on all sorts of topics which were normally taboo when "t'taychers" were about.

If you fancied a spot of entertainment on an otherwise dull evening, you could creep stealthily to the edge of any tent, carefully avoid the taut guy-ropes and crouch down. Recalling days of listening to the wireless when you were younger, you could settle down for thirty minutes of "radio fun" but all laughter had to be carefully stifled.

The lads would comment on a variety of topics: your colleagues on the staff; who had the biggest willy; who could fart the loudest [and longest]; who'd been with the most lasses; who'd had hold of whose tits. The topics were endless in their variety and entertainment value.

Chris's plan revolved around a conversation he'd enjoyed overhearing during his rounds of the tents after Lights Out that night.

A moonlit, eaves-dropping session squatting beside "Nuss" Rowden's tent had given him his idea. He'd returned to the staff tent hot-foot, chortling with glee, as the skeleton of a fun-filled plan formed in his mischievous mind. Now, he gave us a full report of the silently witnessed conversation.

Fat, blond Nuss, the self-proclaimed leader of his Tent Group had been delivering a lecture to his captive audience of Third Year lads:

"Oh, dusta know," Nuss had said, "if tha gets a match an' strikes it, an' tha 'ods it in front of a mirror at midneet...[with an admirable sense of the dramatic delivery] ...*t'Devil comes*. It 'as ter be midneet, o' course, an' tha'r only allowed one match. So who's gorra mirror, eh?"

Gobstruck, incredulous murmurs of wonderment had echoed round the tent, and the rummaging sounds of boys rifling through their belongings in search of mirrors and matches had filtered through the thin canvas. Chris sneaked away as Nuss and the occupants had resolved to wake up at midnight and try it out - "ter see if it's reight..."

Five to midnight finds three highly trained and thoroughly professional teachers creeping silently through the moon-light to take up station immediately outside the Satan Worshippers' tent. Carefully positioning ourselves close by a guy-rope each, we squat and listen in the silence of the North Wales night, straining to catch any noise from the other side of the thin canvas wall.

Not a sound save the hooting of a distant owl on the slate-slopes above the camp, and we are just about to abandon our artful little plot when there is a muffled rumble from deep down inside an adolescent sleeping bag. There are other muffled mutterings and Chris signals thumbs up in the pale moonlight.

"Oh, Nuss! Are ta wakened?"

" 'Course Ah've wakened - an' Ah've getten some matches. 'Oo's getten a mirror?"

"Murphy 'as. 'E sez it's 'is father's shavin'-mirror an' we maun't bust it."

"Reight - gie us it 'ere..."

By now, we highly trained and thoroughly professional teachers have raised ourselves to a semi-crouch, nerves taut and ready for action with a firm two-handed grip on each guy-rope of the tent. We hear the rustlings of others in the tent as they rouse from peaceful slumber to witness the appearance of Beelzebub, and they await with bated breath Nuss's perfomance with mirror and match.

We peer intently at the canvas for any sign of light from the struck match.

" 'Od that mirror still, Murph...Nahthen, are yer all ready fer this," whispers Nuss hoarsely.

There is a faint scrape of the striking match and a weak flame lights up the side of the tent.

At that instant, we shake the guy-ropes with all our might, yelling and hooting like dervishes at the Relief of Lucknow, wailing and screaming like Lucifer himself. From within the tent there is the rushing sound of terror-stricken bowel movements, a mad dash for the tent-door, and eight Shoddy Town lads hurtle out into the moonlight.

Without looking round, they hare off in fear for their very lives towards the dimly-lit latrines, jibbering and slavering in abject terror.

Fat Nuss is last, his pyjama trousers down round his ankles and his pink, wobbly todger trembling with fright in the clear night air. He waddles his terrified fastest and his todger nods staccato-style at the sky as he sprints after the others.

In an instant, they are gone - swallowed up in the Welsh darkness, for all we knew, sprinting towards Penmaenmawr Station, a third class ticket and home to Batley...

But we found them, to our immense professional relief, cowering beside the boundary fence at the bottom of the field, convulsed by the demon-shaking of terror and shock.

We desperately set about using our combined persuasive skills to convince them that there was no reason in this wide world why they shouldn't return to their tent. But for fully two hours they remained clinging to the boundary fence, shaking and shivering in their horrified fright.

They were definitely NOT going back to that tent...

"...In case t'Devil's still theer, sir.... Di'n't y'ear 'im? 'E wor wailing like a stuck pig. Ah wor fair cobbin' bricks, Ah'll tell thi...An' t'tent wouldn't gie o'er shekkin', sir. Ah dadn't go back, sir, - not if me life wor on it..."

What eventually swung them round was the alluring promise [in writing] of double helpings of Rhubarb Crumble and Succulent Camp Custard. All eight occupants of the victimised tent were to be included in the deal and pay-off time would be the very next occasion we guilty teachers were on Kitchen Duty.

We willingly complied, sensing the joke had back-fired somewhat, and as the bedraggled group of teachers and kids traipsed their miserable ways back up the slope, there wasn't one among us who didn't marvel at the amazingly persuasive properties of Dwygyfylchi Pie...

***

EARNING

and LEARNING

If I were to ask you to think of the dirtiest, nastiest, most awful four-letter word you could, then you'd probably come up with the same one as me - WORK. For most of us, "work" casts a daunting shadow over our waking *and* sleeping hours with its ever-present demands. It governs the way we eat, think and behave. It usually gets in the way of having a jolly good time - and, of course, it is *very* necessary...

I bent my student back yet again as I stooped wearily to pick up two more of the frozen lumps which masqueraded as bricks. It was a clear spring day on Rawfolds in Cleckheaton but the overnight frost had bitten hard, and its teeth-marks lingered on in the frozen building materials around me. The bare skin of my fingers stuck to the icy blocks as I loaded them into my heavy black wheelbarrow, each pair of bricks ripping its freeze-welded layer of flesh from my soft, academic palms.

Around me on the site, without a care in the world and oblivious to the chill Cleckheaton air, my predominantly Irish workmates from Connemara, Donegal and County Mayo whistled, sang and swore their happy way through the same task. I pulled my jacket tighter round my chest and longed for a pair of comforting, warm, namby-pamby gloves.

"Why am I subjecting myself to this tortuous anguish?" I ask my inner academic self. Returning from my comfortable London existence only two days ago in early April, 1964, why didn't I take time to live the life of Riley for a day or two, idling my time away in the Yew Tree or the bookies' down our road?

The answer, in a word was ... *Brass.*

Without it, there was no way I could go out and have a good time! So, just for the vacation, I'd subjected myself to the rampant blight which gallops through our daily lives for thirty or so years, until we hang up our boots and make for the garden-seat and the home-brewed ale.

Looking back, I'm glad that I went out of my way to do as many different jobs as possible while it didn't matter so much. What I didn't realise then was that work was an important part of my education in "learning about Life" as they say. On that score, my *real* education had actually begun a few years before, at the bottom of Stone Street, close to the Punchbowl public house...

At the early age of fifteen and filled with adolescent awe, I take up my first proper job at P&C Garnett Limited [Textile Machine Makers] Cleckheaton. Sporting my set of regulation navy-blue overalls, I make my anxious way into "the machine shop" and marvel at the cacophonous din of a horde of metal-cutting machines grinding out their daily quota of machine parts.

My youthful sense of wonder is compounded by the discovery that one of the most important skills at work turns out to be the art of clock-watching. Everybody seemed to be obsessed by the passage of time.

Present yourself at at 7.30am in front of a clock and clock on/in; work till mid-day and clock off/out. With a full belly, return to the self-same spot and clock on/in again. Experience the daily ecstatic delight of clocking off/out at 5pm and hare off up Stone Street as if the farmer's gun is but two inches from your arse-end.

But clock-watching didn't finish at that. Oh no! You see, the clock was an integral part of every single one of your daily tasks as it cast its threatening shadow over each work-place in the entire establishment.

I well remember that first day on the shop-floor, grinding Mudrick spikes. Following a quick demonstration by the diminutive Irishman, Tommy Fanning who milled them, I had to sharpen those three-inch spikes on a five-inch grinding wheel. They were for a Mudrick roller which would eventually find its mechanical way onto a giant Garnett Rag-grinding machine. So every time you've

127

filled a bag with 500 sharpened spikes, clock a card and tie it to the khaki-coloured sack. Then the job can be costed up by the clerks in the Works Office.

Exciting? Well it was for the first fifteen minutes or so, because I enjoyed making those spikes as sharp as needle-points and sending a shower of colourful sparks all over the Machine-Shop floor, like lighting fireworks in the street on Mischief Night. I was so engrossed in my work that when the buzzer went for the 8.50am breakfast break and the mighty machine roar fell silent for ten minutes, Yours Truly was still playing at fireworks!

I was quite disappointed when the other machinists shouted at me scornfully: "Sit dahn, young 'un, an' get thisen a pot o' teea..."

After the first two hours or so, I have to say that the job lost a good deal of its initial charm. I became so efficient at sharpening those spikes that my mind switched off and I fell to glancing over my shoulder at the big brass time-clock on the Machine Shop wall to see how many minutes had passed.

"Reight," I would say to myself. "Ah'm offter do thirty spikes afore Ah look at yon bloody clock ageean. That'll be twenty minutes easy..."

"... twenty-nine, thirty." Casual glance at the clock. "FIVE minutes??? The bloody thing must 'a' stopped!"
Oh, how the time dragged!

The only relief came in the occasional conversation with my work-mates about football, ale and - or so it seemed to me at the time - the very popular pastime of 'leg-over'. Every exchange of views along such lines was brought to a perfunctory conclusion with a careful consideration of the works clock and the joyful revelation that twenty or so minutes of the firm's time had been taken - at no significant cost to the borrower.

I put it all down to the fact that we had to 'clock in/on' and 'clock out/off' in order to get that little brown envelope of treasure trove on Thursday afternoons. The sum total of its contents was calculated entirely by reference to the brown card in the rack next to the time-clock at the works' entrance.

Throughout my first week, naively mis-reading the numbers on the great wooden rack, I took the *wrong* card to clock in/on and out/off. It felt good to shove it deftly into the slot, to hear the 'ding' to say that it had been time-punched, and to replace it in the rack.

So, during that week, upon arrival at work, some poor bugger must have taken his card from the rack and said to himself: "Hell's Buckets! Ah'm already 'ere!" Worse still, at leaving time: "Well, bugger me! Ah must bi 'alf way ooam bi nah!"

I discovered my mistake on the following Thursday when brown-smocked Mr Harry Howarth came round with the little wooden tray and the neatly arranged pay packets. As he neared my machine, I watched him eagerly, ready to grab my hard-earned packet of treasure-trove. But to my dismay, he by-passed me altogether.

An hour or so later, plucking up all my adolescent courage, I knocked sheepishly on the Foreman's Office door and politely enquired as to the whereabouts of my hard-earned cash. Somewhat puzzled, Harry H. sets off for the Office to investigate the matter...

Eventually, he returns and makes a summary statement: "Oh... tha dunt get paid if tha dunt clock on, tha knows." With a solemn face, he produces my buff-coloured time-card from behind his back.

There is my name and *there* is my number but, to my dismay, none of the time-spaces have been purple-stamped. It shows a completely blank week.

"Burr Ah've clocked mi card all week, Mr Howarth! 'Onest, Ah 'ave!"

I was dismissed with a stern stare and a "Don't-give-me-that-excuse" look. Crestfallen and penniless, I turned back to my grinding-wheel. A week's worth of fireworks and razor-sharp spikes - all for nowt!

But Mr Howarth was a real gent, and he called me back. " 'Ere," he said as he produced the treasure-trove from behind his back. "Ah've sorted it aht fer thi - An' next week, see as tha learns ter read."

He grinned mischievously as he tapped me lightly on the head with my little brown packet before tucking it into the top pocket of my overalls...

*

By far the happiest job I had was on the building sites of the Heavy Woollen District, working with people who enriched my college life with their earthy humour and worldly wisdom: "When tha works Sunday on a Monday, it feels like Tuesday."

For some reason, I was honoured by acceptance into their ranks and not tagged - like so many others - as a "useless student twat".

I drank my tea from a bucket-sized tea-cup which was the envy of the whole gang, referring to the spent leaves in the bottom as "rat-shit". I broke out concrete flooring with a jack-hammer [pneumatic drill], dug holes and laid 'consolidated consecration' [wire-reinforced concrete] with the finest of men. I ate my 'snap' in various navvies' huts, read the Daily Mirror and swore with the best of them.

Life was simple and straight-forward - dig all day and drink all night, the pressures of academic life far removed - floating away on some distant London horizon - until my return in October.

I was privileged to work alongside Joe Conway from Connemara, a master of ready wit and repartee. Spotting my weedy white torso one fine summer afternoon, he was moved to instruct me: "Put on yer shirt, me boy, afore the flies get at ye." And I shovelled for the waist-coated Peter Leary from Donegal who slept in digs above the Malt Shovel in Cleckheaton, took breakfast in the White Rose Cafe and spent the rest of his leisure time in the Saloon Bar, drinking pints of Guinness till his eyes went red and he floundered his way upstairs to bed.

At fairly frequent intervals, whilst digging or shovelling, Peter would lift one foot onto his shovel, lean heavily on the handle and shout: "Relax! Let Capstan* take the strain," thus airing the suggestion that we might consider stopping work, lean likewise on our shovels and take a hard-earned smoke-break.

One of the pleasures of this job was demolition.

We were frequently detailed to pull down a wall, dig up a concrete floor or smash out wooden window frames. Such tasks required a great deal of strength and little thought, so I was ideally suited - young, fit and true of eye! But I was totally unprepared for meeting the other labourers who made up the demolition gangs and who spent almost their entire waking existence smashing things up and burning great piles of waste on huge smoking bonfires...

Bill and Albert were bosom buddies in the wrecking trade and, on the day I first met them, they had both been newly appointed to their present posts of responsibility - pulling down an old drying shed at a local mill. They had both recently completed their respective stays in Armley Jail for previous offences, committed separately but punished coincidentally.

With strong, square jaws and tattooed from arse to elbow, they frightened the living daylights out of me without even uttering a word, such was the ferocity of their glare.

When they spoke, their talk was liberally scattered with vivid invective derived from their life in prison, and it regularly threatened abuse to anyone who might get in their way - including me.

Wiry, weasel-faced Bill discovered one day that I was training to be a teacher and he immediately began to philosophise, casting threatening, accusing looks at me.

"Oh so tha'r bahna be a taycher, ar ta," he growled menacingly.

---

*   Capstan Medium   a leading brand of cigarette in the 50' and 60's

                                      every cigarette bearing the signature:

                                      "W.D. & H. O. Wills"

"Well, what Ah wanna know is this: 'Ow come we 'adter call all t' f...... taychers '*Sir*'? Ah mean, they're ner better ner us, ar' they? Tha'r ner better ner me, ar' ta?"

Nodding vigorously, I readily agreed with this carefully considered view. Lying about needing a pee and having left my Woodbines in my jacket pocket, I shot round the back of the shed in a cold sweat. By the time I returned, about five minutes later, Bill had already forgotten the line of our discussion and was happily enveloped in clouds of thickening dust as he used the compressor to break down a wall. Saved by the jack-hammer!

Albert was a huge blond-haired man and, I discovered, a gentle giant - until he was roused. He'd been detained at Armley as the result of a GBH charge, but avowed that it hadn't been his fault. The other chap had helped himself to Albert's pint from the bar and Albert had 'accidentally' bumped into him on the way back "fro' t'piss-oil". A carelessly placed bar-stool had somehow found its way into Albert's hand as he defended himself against the onslaught from "t'other bloke" who had ended the evening in Batley Hospital.

Bill and Albert remain vividly etched on my memory because, along with them, I became a thief! Now before you get me wrong,I didn't fall into house-breaking or robbery-with-violence in order to supplement my student grant. No - I was "encouraged" by my two work-mates to indulge in some petty pilfering from the firm - the sort that most people get up to at some time during their working life. It's simple to commit because you're not actually pinching from any *person*; your victim has no other identity than "Them", so this makes it a bit easier on your conscience...

One bright summer's morning, about half-an-hour into our day's toil - wrecking the inside of an old dye-house - Albert let out a massive cry of glee: "Chopper! Ey oop, Bill! These 'eaters is full o' chopper!" ['Chopper' I learned, was building-site slang for copper - a valuable and nickable commodity.]

Now at this particular building firm, it was accepted practice that any finds of scrap metal unearthed on wrecking jobs such as this were to be slung aside in a corner for collection at the end of the day. All such scrap would then be weighed in for cash with the local scrap-dealer at a later date. We had a pretty good idea as to the destination of such cash as we enviously eyed the Boss's sleek, brown Bentley saloon with its registration mark *ARC 1*.

It didn't take Bill and Albert long to discover that there were upwards of twenty of the industrial-sized roof-hung heaters, and that each one contained fifteen or so finned copper tubes. With pick and shovel, they set about dismantling each heater and gleefully watched the pile of salvaged copper grow.

Now, did they think of throwing the copper in a corner for collection later in the day? Was it their copper, to do with as they pleased? Did they consider weighing in some of it for themselves at Gypsy Jack's, the local scrap-dealer? I'll leave you to guess the answer to these questions as you picture the following scene:

Bill and Albert, devoting all their combined and concentrated energies to extracting every last ounce of 'chopper' from the twenty or so heaters. Yours Truly, detailed by Albert, as follows:

1. to continue with the 'proper' work of the day so as to create a cloud of dust in order to conceal the true nature of their activity

2. to keep a look-out for anybody in authority

3. to create a pile of rubbish under which the stolen 'chopper' might be concealed overnight [This was going to be a long job]

Indeed, the activity lasted for well over a week and by the following Tuesday, we had a veritable mountain of copper hidden away in one corner of the site. But there was a problem.

As Bill succinctly put it: "'Ow the 'Ell ar we bahna gerrit ter Gypsy Jack's? We 'aven't a wagon or owt."

But Albert was equal to such a challenging question: "On t'bus - there's one ev'ry quarter-an-'our."

Of course, the use of public transport for the carriage of our illicit haul of copper had to be a top-secret operation. So the very next day, as part of our cunning plan to exchange the contraband for ready cash, we all arrived at work in sweltering sunshine wearing our raincoats and overalls. And at the end of the working day, we took our coats and loaded them with as much of the shiny copper as we could.

We carefully stuffed lengths of it down trouser-legs, into sleeve-holes and up our jacket-linings. Painstakingly, we bent and folded pieces of the precious metal and secreted them deftly about our persons. After a great deal of sweating and grunting, Albert even managed to sling some in the pouch of his Y-fronts.

Half an hour of intricate, industrious packing passed by, and we hauled on our clothing, ready to clank our way to the bus-stop. We were unable to bend any of our important bodily bits in order to perform the simple task of walking, and we shambled along like Lon Chaney look-alikes from those early Frankenstein movies.

When the number 64 from Bradford town centre arrived, it took three Tin Men all of five minutes to climb aboard. We helped each other to drag our immense carcasses onto the platform. Albert, dripping sweat like a two year old filly at Ascot, immediately made for the upper deck - where he could "'ave a fag."

Bill's whispered hiss of an instruction stopped him in his tracks:

"'Ow ar ta bahna gerrup theer, yer daft twat???" He indicated an empty seat on the lower deck with a contorted nod of his head, his arm immobilised by raincoat sleeves full of heavy metal. "Downstairs..."

We took up residence on the lower deck, each of us occupying a double seat with our legs stretched out stiffly into the aisle. Any remonstration from the conductor was stifled in mid-throat by Albert's threatening glare and bunched fist, and he took our fares in obsequious Uriah Heep fashion.

After a further circus of groaning contortions and heavy metal movement, we alighted the No. 64 at Gypsy Jack's in the old Station Approach. I stood at a respectful distance while the two experts handled the deal in the dark and dirty wooden shed at the far end of the yard.

After five minutes of shaking heads and earnest consultation with the swarthy, ear-ringed proprietor of the scrap metal business, we all undressed and 'weighed in' our treasure, relieved to be rid of our cumbersome loads. Shifty looks and whispered remarks were exchanged before Bill called me over.

"'Ere - this is thine..." He passed me a beautiful, brown, wrinkled ten-bob note. Then, with a menacing curl of his top lip and a knowing grimace: "... an' tha keeps thi f...... gob shut. *Reight*??"

And I have, Bill. To this day, I swear, I have, Bill...

The pinnacle of my building-site career arrived one hot and sticky August afternoon in 1966, when I experienced the ultimate triumph of being put in charge of two men and my own hole.

Desperately grasping at straws to staff the many jobs which had cropped up at the local woollen mill where we were permanently based, Joe Dickinson, the site foreman, rounded a factory corner and made for the gang of three I was currently assisting to lay concrete flooring.

Dougie was a young desperado, fresh out of prison, slow of wit and suffering a permanent nasal complaint so that all his remarks were preceded by a deep catarrh-clearing sniff. Grey haired, arthritic George was 'knocking on' in building-site terms and was retained by the firm as a loyal labourer who was now only good for light work, making tea and fetching things from the shop. And there was Yours Truly - twenty years old, still wet behind the ears, but strong enough to wield a pick and shovel.

"Oh! You three! Get thisens over 'ere," was the foreman's polite initial request. "Ah've a job fo' thi." Removing his cap and scratching the back of his head, Joe outlines our mission instructions:

"Gerrover inter t'cardin' oil an' brek some floor aht in t'corner office. It's all marked aht fo' thi an' tha'll need t'compressor, so tek t'dumper an' gerrit rahnd."

He paused thoughtfully, his gaze passing from George to Dougie and coming to rest on me. With a faraway look in his eye, he sniffed wistfully.

"Nahthen, Freddie," he said. "Thee keep an eye on t'job, will ta? If owt goes wrong, Ahs'll blame thee." He shrugged his ageing shoulders, donned his headgear and walked off, contemplating the floor and shaking his head despairingly.

The others looked enquiringly at me with a *'What-shall-we-do-next, Gaffer?'* expression on their dull faces. Grasping the nettle and taking complete charge, I issued my first and only instruction: "Relax! Let Capstan take the strain!"

*

By far the most frightening job I ever did was working for a local security firm which I shall call 'Plantguards'. After responding to an advert in the local evening paper, I was interviewed for all of ten minutes one summer's evening in a city-centre office by a bespectacled, middle-aged chap in uniform. Then, I was rushed downstairs, kitted out with an old police uniform [complete with truncheon] and told to get a passport-sized photograph for my ID Card - pretty damn quick.

Less than seven days later, I was a fully-fledged Security

Officer, sitting in the tiny office-entrance to one of the largest mail-order stores in the country. It's the wee small hours and I'm guarding many thousands of pounds-worth of highly nickable gear!

Now, I don't know about you, but sitting alone in the dark has never been one of my strong points. I made sure that I'd got plenty of lights switched on to deter potential thieves and I also had an ample stock of reading material to while away the night.

In those days, the wireless stations closed down at 2am, so I was well set up, I thought, for a comfortable night's work. Lots of strip-lights beaming bright would say to those snooping robbers: "Piss off, mate. There's somebody in here [armed and dangerous], so tek yer 'ook!"

But when the patrolling Sergeant visited me at the beginning of my twelve hour stint and told me to switch off all the lights and to operate by torchlight, I was somewhat disappointed. And when he informed me that I would not be exercising my arse-muscles in an easy chair all night whilst reading a book, I was quite taken aback.

You see, what I had to do was carry a special clock around with me on a shoulder-strap as I toured the entire store. I was to find keys chained to walls in strategic places - in dark corners and behind locked doors - and insert them into my clock. One complete turn was required in order to print a time on a paper-tape inside the clock to prove that I'd been on my rounds.

I had to complete eight rounds during the night and ring in to HQ after each round to report that all was well.

At unspecified times throughout my shift, a patrolling sergeant would call in to unlock my clock with his special key and check the tape to see that I'd done my rounds, as stated on my log-sheet [to be completed by me].

Not quite the easy life I'd expected, but one which taught me a great deal about myself in the character/courage field: i.e. throughout my period of employment with

Plantguards, I worked in a permanent state of trouser-filling terror! Not only was I guarding very valuable and highly-nickable goodies - jewellery, electrical goods, guns - I was utterly and entirely all on my own.

At three o'clock in the morning, when the streets outside are deathly silent and the whole of the honest population of the city is fast asleep, the creeping feeling of loneliness is nothing less than devastating. And when you have to make your way by torchlight round the vast building, between dark alleys of high ranged shelves, expecting to be jumped on by a Bill Sykes burglar at every dark corner as you stop to clock your tape, the combination of abject terror and miserable loneliness leads to severe toilet difficulties, I can tell you!

On one particular shift, at about three in the morning, I'm about to leave the comfort of my cosy little safe-haven of the office to execute a tour of the building. I carefully mark the page in my novel, strap on my clock and don my Plantguards peaked cap.

I am just about to lock the office-door when I hear the loud crash of breaking glass about twenty yards down the corridor.

After clawing my heart back from somewhere near the ceiling and wiping away rivers of sweat from my pulsating forehead, the true grit and spirit of the Plantguard in me came to the fore: "Wait here for half an hour, Fred, then do a tour of the building. By that time, any robbers breaking and entering will have filled their swag-bags and buggered off, leaving you to discover a theft. Ring in to HQ and report incredulously, using all your amateur theatrical skills: "Sarge! There's been a robbery and I never heard a thing! Not a sound, Sarge, honest...."

Thirty minutes later, as arranged with myself, and with pulsating tremors of fear wracking my entire body, I crept out of the office to complete my tour. I found .... nothing!

All was in order. No windows had been broken, no safes cracked, no jewellery swiped. There was no Bill Sykes lurking behind a storage rack ready to beat in my skull. The entire establishment was in apple-pie order, waiting silently for the beginning of the next working day. The loud crash I had heard must remain a mystery forever, like "*The Marie Celeste*" ...

As you've probably guessed, the biggest draw-back to this particular job was that there was never anybody to talk to, with whom to share your fears. The only conversation you might have throughout the entire lonely, twelve hour shift might be with the visiting Patrol Sergeant who would dive out of his white van with its "Plantguard" insignia, sprint to your clock to check your tape and sprint out again in a flash of light, with the inevitable words: "See yer, mate. Ah've twelve more ter do afore t'end o' t'shift."

He would then shatter the silence of the dead-of-night streets with a Le Mans engine-roar and a pall of blue exhaust smoke as he made off into the enveloping darkness.

Yes, looking back on it, the worst thing about being a Plantguard was that I was *always* on my own - except for that time when they gave me a dog...

It was a week-end shift, guarding a compound full of British Road Services lorries, loaded up the previous Friday night for Monday morning deliveries. Nobody ever informed me as to the contents of the lorries, but you can guess that they must have been pretty valuable - enough for the company to fork out hard earned cash for Plant-guards to watch over them for the entire week-end.

I worked all this out for myself when, early on in my shift, a sergeant arrived with a lean and hungry-looking, cross-eyed Alsatian dog. In official company language, he announced that this animal was to assist me in the conduct of my duties. Before streaking off in the usual pall of blue exhaust smoke, he left me with sketchy instructions on how to employ the beast on my rounds, along with two tins of dog food and a doggie dish.

To this day, I still do not know what I should have done after the Guy Fawkes Night warning had been issued to would-be assassins: "Stand still, or I'll let the dog off!" And I gave the matter little thought, pleased now because I had another "being" with which to converse.

Not having been informed of the canine's title, I invested it with the imaginative and highly original name of "Dog".

To this, it responded in a friendly and tail-wagging manner, so I had a fellow life-force with which to pass the time. Now as it happened, this was a day-shift, so at least the next poor bugger would have the dog for company throughout the long dark night.

But for the present, I've decided that it's time for a round of the perimeter fence, clocking the afore-mentioned keys, which were attached to some of the twelve-foot high steel posts.

The sun was shining on a pleasant Saturday afternoon, Dog was obedient enough with basic commands whenever I had to stop at a key and clock my tape, and, all things considered, this was one of the easier of my Plantguards assignments.

Making my way to the first of the many keys, I ambled across the wide open space of the compound, babbling on to Dog at my side. For a few moments at least, I felt briefly at peace with the world.

As I stopped at the first key and proceeded about my business, some scruffy young kids from the High Moor estate were enjoying a kick-about in the field on the other side of the perimeter fence. Feeling protected by a twelve-foot, chain-link see-through screen and being Estate Kids, they dared to enter into some gentle banter with the Young Security Guard and his Dog:

"What a mangey looking dog," shouted Estate Kid One, a round-faced bespectacled ten year-old fatty. "I berrit's got fleas."

"It looks too freetened to do owt. Ah berrit shits itsen when it sees a robber," shouted Estate Kid Two, a lanky lad with freckles, catching on to his mate's bravado.

Estate Kids Three to Seven giggled and tittered at such brazen cheek and shaped up to join in the fun.

"Hey, that's enough of that talk, young man," I scolded in my sternest teacher-voice, whilst secretly agreeing with their assessment of my guardian animal.

"Piss off, mister" sneered the fatty [Estate Kid One] and he kicked the ball as hard as he could at the fencing. I ducked involuntarily and Dog yelped in fright.

Now, as a result of their chum's derring-do, numbers Two to Seven proceeded to shout and scream at my canine companion. At this, Dog's upper lip curled to reveal yellow vicious-looking fangs, and he began straining at the leash and barking hysterically.

To his credit, Dog was stronger than his mangey appearance led me to believe, and he was soon up on his hind legs, front paws on the chain-link fencing, ready to tear some little kid limb from limb.

Such a display of potential harm did not deter our Estate Heroes, however. From a safe distance of two or three yards, protected by the 12-foot fence they continued a stream of filthy abuse, aimed principally at Dog but occasionally directed at "that lanky bastard in his silly uniform..."

After all, they were quite safe from any vengeful act on the part of Dog or Yours Truly.

By now, I'd had enough of being insulted by ones so young, and,adopting an official sounding Plantguards tone, I issued the standard warning: "*Stand still, or I'll let the dog off!*"

"So f...... what," shouted the fatty, really chancing his arm now with his Estate Kids' vocabulary. He came right up to the fence and flicked a V-sign at me and Dog - with both hands! And the others soon cottoned on, joining in to form a raucous line of nine and ten year olds, all flicking V-signs, dancing like little cannibals and chorusing rhythmically:

"F... off, mister,

An' thi f...... dog."

My hand had been called and there was nothing for it but to let Dog have his freedom.

When they realised that it was free to roam, and when they caught a closer glimpse of those yellow, dripping fangs, those Estate Kids would streak off into the distance, never to be seen again. And I'd be left in peace.

I slipped the lead and issued the next standard command: "GO!"

Dog hurtled himself at the fencing, barking viciously and snarling devilishly, but Estate Heroes didn't stop. They carried on as before, chanting even louder to outdo Dog's frantic howling. Sensing that the jape had gone too far, I decided to call Dog in and abandon any further attempt at discipline through fear. But there were two inherent problems in this course of action:

1. No standard command for recall of Dog had been issued. No matter what I shouted, Dog continued his howling frenzy.

2. Dog found a loose flap of fencing which had been damaged by other Estate Kids, no doubt trying to break in while former Plantguards' backs had been turned.

Somehow, Dog wriggled and writhed through this smallest of gaps under the fence and made off in a frenzy of snarls and yapping in pursuit of the gang. In the seconds that it took him to get under the fence, Estate Kids One to Seven realised the serious threat now posed by the insensed brute. As a man, they took to their tiny little heels and ran. Hotly pursued by slavering Dog, they tore off up the slope towards the safety of their Estate and Home. In desperation, I searched the nether reaches of my brain for any command which might effect the return of Dog: "Come back! Heel! Come in! Come by! Here, you dozy bastard of an animal!"

I tried them all, but none of them worked. Eight small dark shapes [including Dog] disappeared over the Saturday afternoon horizon into the setting sun as it silhouetted the roof-tops of High Moor.

An eerie and awesome silence descended, as I peered into the distance, straining my ears for the awful sound of tearing Estate Kids' flesh in the inevitable ensuing slaughter...

About an hour later, a six-foot bull of a Dad, clad in his vest, displaying a vividly tattooed torso and looking remarkably like Estate Kid One, shook the perimeter fence in order to secure my attention.

"Oi - thee! Lanky twat! Dusta know that thy dog's bin pesterin' my lad, so Ah've rung t'bobbies an' they've tekken it away!"

Not wishing to enter into any lengthy discussion with the Incredible Estate Hulk on the matter, I thanked him kindly for his concern, assured him that it wouldn't happen again and began to back away sheepishly towards the safety of the compound office behind me.

"It better not 'appen ageean Ah'll tell thi', else Ahs'll come over yon fence an' sort thee an' thi f...... dog aht " were Estate Hulk's concluding remarks as he shambled back to "The Iron Man" to finish his evening pint and game of darts.

I made my trembling way back to the compound office to ponder Dog's whereabouts over a nice hot cup of tea...

A few days passed and sadly, I never saw Dog again because of "The Vocabulary Incident" which involved my inefficient use of a password.

"Come Back! Heel! Come in! Come by!"

You see, presumably because I was a raw and new recruit, and presumably because they were desperate for unsuspecting personnel to do such a lousy job anyway, nobody in the Plantguard Operations Room had seen fit to let me in on the Company Policy if ever you were confronted by robbers on the job, so to speak. I discovered the know-how by accident, one lonely, early dawn when a Patrol Sergeant called Derek chose to stop with me for a five-minute cup of tea...

After my anxious enquiry about the regularity of night-time robberies involving Plantguards staff, Derek gasped incredulously. " 'As nob'dy telled yer what ter do if ever they gerrin??? What a carry-on! Well, what tha does is this..." and he proceeded to clue me in...

"They gerrin an' start threatenin' an' that, an' you *say:* *"Tha can do what tha likes, owd lad, but if Ah dooant ring HQ in t'next ten minutes, shit'll 'it t'fan and t'patrols and t'bobbies'll be all over 'ere - so tha'd best let me ring in"...* "An' they say *"Aye.... Reight.... But no monkey business, mind, else tha cops it..."""*

"So tha rings in, an' when 'e answers t'phone, t'Desk Sergeant allus asks thi if tha'r alreight - an' that's when tha slips 'im t'password, dusta see?"

Cottoning on swiftly to such a complicated strategy, I nodded knowingly. "So all I need to know is the password, then?"

"Reight enough," retorts Derek. "An' Ahs'll tell thi..."

With a dramatic edge to his voice, he announced: "Tha sez: *"Aye, Ah'm IN THE PINK!"* - 'cos that's thi password, tha sees - " *IN THE PINK*". Now, as soon as t'Sergeant 'ears this, 'e tells all units to get over to wherever tha 'appens ter be - an' 'e tells t'bobbies, an' all".

At this point, Derek sucks in his cheeks in a knowing manner. "An' believe you me, young 'un, they come like shit off a shovel. All tha as ter do is keep 'em talkin' or even lerrem gerron wi' t'job. Next thing tha knows, t'place is surrounded - an' tha'r safe."

This was great news indeed! To think that the vast back-up team and the entire organisation of Plantguards had been behind me all the time, ready to take instant action if ever I were to be threatened by nasty robbers! And the whole machinery would leap into efficient, decisive action - all with the use of three little words. It was very reassuring to know, I can tell you!

So Patrol Sergeant Derek drained the dregs of his very early-morning tea from his cup, waved me a cheery goodbye and departed for the next call on his rounds. Shaking my head in wonderment at the complexities of security arrangements, I locked the door behind him, and returned to the snug little office and my thriller novel: "I'm in the pink! Fancy, a simple little idea like that! Amazing! Brilliant!" I marvelled to myself...

Several nights later, guarding the large mail order store again, I was so far into a thriller novel that I failed to notice the office clock ticking its way through the wee small hours. In a panic, off I shot on a round of clocking keys, knowing that I was a bit late ringing in to report that all was well. The first streaks of grey dawn light were beginning to wash the dark sky - a welcome sign that heralded the end of the shift in a couple of hours or so, and the joyful release into a bright new morning.

I returned breathless to the office, my mind obviously somewhere between the thriller in which I'd been engrossed and the delicious prospect of going home to bed. Pleasant thoughts were buzzing round my brain-box as I reached for the telephone...

I dutifully and somewhat hastily rang the HQ number, gave my location and Job Number and received kind, concerned Desk Sergeant's standard greeting: "Narthen lad, are y'awreight?"

"Aye," says I, absently. "I'm fine - I'm in the pink, thank you," and I returned to my novel.

Within five minutes, the early-morning silence was blasted by a furious bashing on the great front door of the entrance. I opened up and a posse of Plantguard Sergeants and PC Flatfoots charged past me, accompanied by several yelping and baying alsatian dogs. "Where are they, the bastards - lemme at 'em," shouted the Sergeant in charge, brandishing his shiny black truncheon. "We'll show the twats..."

After my feeble explanation, the language of my official dismissal from the Plantguards organisation was succinct: "Piss off, mate; and don't bother coming back..."

And do you know, I never did! Instead, I ended up in a classroom, dealing with Estate Kids for thirty years. It was great fun, but it didn't teach me half as much about Life as had Harry Howarth, Peter Leary, Patrol Sergeant Derek or, for that matter, his Dog.

**

ALTERNATIVE  MEDICINE

Yet another rapier blade of searing pain shot down my leg as I attempted my teacher's strut [like you do] around the sunlit classroom. Without giving anything away to the class of Fourth year kids who were enjoying my story about Grandad's Petrol Pump Calamity, I ambled in anguish to the front and gingerly eased my foot up onto the front edge of Cooky's desk. He wasn't too impressed at my gymnastics, but it made for an interesting and static final five minutes of the lesson.

As my charges left the room to the fading clang of the four o'clock bell, I was the subject of one or two meaningfully enquiring glances, not having moved a muscle for the last eight or nine minutes...

Feeling like a nonagenarian, I staggered painfully over to my desk and began to indulge in some confidence boosting dialogue with myself:

"Now just think on, lad and listen...

1. *You're still young enough to play cricket and football despite smoking and drinking a fair quantity.*

2. *You're earning a good weekly packet by applying a vigorous amount of energy to your daily toil.*

3. *You're sensible enough to be married and weighed down with a mortgage for the next twenty five years.*

So you're not old in the Old Gipper sense of the word. But is it the dreaded passage of Anno Domini which is creating these needle-stabs of pain which have been shooting down your leg for the last six months? And why do you have to twist and contort your body every ten minutes for the relief thereof?"

Answering myself decisively, I resolved there and then to take evasive action to get things sorted out before I got *really* old. More especially so, because this infernal pain in my leg had begun to prevent my active weekly, and youthfully enthusiastic involvement on the football fields of Division Three of the West Riding Old Boys' League...

"Now this is your problem, Mr Butler...." murmured Mr Bidwell, the Back Specialist, as he extracted the X-ray pictures of my dorsal bits from a large oak drawer in his large oak-panelled desk. His deep voice echoed round his large oak-panelled consulting room as he tucked away my fat cheque [by way of his consultancy fee] in the side-pocket of his large oak-panelled wallet.

He smiled benignly down at me as I lay prone on the medical couch.

"You see, you have congenital damage to the lumbar vertebrae causing fusion in this area *here*, which in turn causes compression of the cartilaginous tissue *here*, and produces pressure on the sciatic nerve *here*. This causes the pain down *here*, which you already know about..."

With each "*here*", he flicked his silver-topped fountain pen over the pale grey X-ray pictures, like Kenneth More organising a night raid on Hanover in one of those pale-grey Saturday afternoon war films. When he came to the edge of the picture, he proceeded to indicate the bomb targets down my leg.

I nodded wisely, earnestly contemplating my thigh, understanding his drift about my present complaint but not really interested until he got to the bit about the cure.

"And what it means is this..." he drawls.

"You will have to stop work for six months, spend as much time as possible lying down and you will have to wear a specially made steel corset to immobilise your lumbar region. If this fails to correct the complaint, we shall have to operate - and I'm afraid the track record of success in these cases is not good..."

149

"Does this mean that I shall have to stop playing football," I ask forlornly.

"Oh, Good God, man! I very much doubt that you'll ever play again."

I made my shattered way home in a state of utter and abject depression. Missing work for six months I could stand. The prospect of being at home on my back, encased in metal, was tolerable.

But no more football?? *That* thought was too awful to contemplate. Whatever was I going to do?

The answer to this last question was a long time in coming and in the meantime, I "soldiered on", writhing and twisting my body into various contortions to gain some respite from the agonising pain down my leg. My young charges were somewhat amused as their teacher taught them, sometimes with one leg up on the front desk-top, sometimes bent double like an old hag, but always with a sour grimace of pain across his young [ish] face.

Friends on the football field were less tolerant.

I soon became known as "Badback" Butler in the Wheel-wright Old Boys AFC Third XI, and had to take a prolonged lay-off from the beautiful game, pending further enquiries and the quest for treatment.

Now, the strange phenomenon surrounding a bit of back trouble is that everybody [and his mother] has had a touch of it at some time in their lives, and thus has the ready solution to all your problems at their finger-tips. This they proceed to ram down your unsuspecting throat at every available opportunity...

"Garlic pills and plenty of roughage," somebody said. This remedy resulted in frequent and regular trips to the toilet.

"Nettle tea and plenty of Vitamin b2" [to be taken in close proximity to a toilet].

"Sit in front of a heat lamp and rub on Fiery Jack ointment, but keep it well away from your important bits."

"Sleep with a board under t'mattress lad, but look out for woodworm."

"Sit in a hot salty bath full of comfrey leaves, with your knees under your chin and your hands cupped round your knackers..."

In desperation, I tried all the suggested remedies to no avail. Yet another football season melted into glorious summer and still, it seemed, there was no immediate hope of ever playing regularly again.

I'd just about begun to dismally and reluctantly accept the Specialist's diagnosis when old Norman Hepworth mentioned to me one day in the staff room that he'd had a recurrence of *his* back-trouble. It had reared its ugly head at the week-end when he'd been attempting to extract a particularly stubborn leek in his allotment. "So I shall have to go to my *Osteopath* and get it sorted," he grimaced, clutching the back of a chair for support.

At the mention of cures for bad backs, my ears prick up. One telephone call and a few days later, I'm making my way along a back street in Bradford for an expensive session with Norman's highly recommended *Osteopath*.

This bloke's consultancy venue is his front room which is just a touch off-putting when you're paying for a "medical" consultation. However, I resolutely fight my way past coats, wellies and a viciously yapping fox terrier in the hallway, before entering the "Consulting Room".

The Osteopath is a tall, lugubrious chap with greying hair and a thin angular face. He solemnly requests that I lie down on a large settee and enters "psychoanalyst" mode as he quizzes me about my current condition. Copious notes are made in a little green pocket book and, upon payment of the requisite fee, I am invited to return at the same time next week.

In desperation and the fervent hope of a cure, I continue my treatment for a couple of months or so, kissing bye-bye to many pounds sterling in the process. Divested of clothing save for Y-fronts and socks, I am bent, yanked and heated up in the dorsal area. The thought of playing Division Three Yorkshire Old Boys' football the following season drives me to extreme lengths of utter dedication, but it is all to no avail. At the end of my course of treatment, lightning jabs of pain are still shooting down to my ankle and I continue to teach with one leg up. So for the time being at any rate, the quest is abandoned...

A chance conversation in a pub with an old cricketing companion, however, and hope springs afresh. "A mate o' mine 'ad t'self-same bother, an' 'e went to a feller in Batley Carr wi' an 'ammer. 'Alf a dollar, it cost 'im, but, tha knows, e's as reight as a bobbin nar..."

Intrigued as to the medical purpose of a hammer in the curative process and desperate to at least stand on the touch-line for the 1971-72 season, I learned that no appointment system was in operation to see the said "feller".

"Tha just 'as ter queue up and wait thi turn."

The summer sun filters wanly through the grime and dust of Bradford Road as I scurry through the gloom and shadows beneath the dark and looming satanic mills. I reach a steepling side-street of terraced houses at the top of which there is, indeed, a long queue outside number thirty six. Most of the occupants of the queue are older than me and sport flat-caps and blue industrial overalls, so I feel a bit out of place in my schoolmaster's uniform. But I'm here now and this back-street physician just might be the answer to my problems. Besides which, I want to know about that hammer. I shelve my doubts and join the line...

A public-convenience stream of flat-capped and overalled figures enters and leaves number thirty six. Upon his exit to the cobbled pavement, each "patient" flexes his muscles and stretches the offending limb with a knowing wink and a grin at the remaining occupants of the queue. I soon sense a growing optimism about standing on the touchline during the coming season.

Reaching the head of the line, I sneak a look into the house and, to my dismay, I catch sight of another dark hallway and another canine occupant - this time a fat, smelly, black Labrador sprawling across the width of the narrow hall, slavering all over the dull brown linoleum.

At last, it's my turn. I boldly circumnavigate the dog and enter another dark and dingy front room for my consultation with the physician who is bending over an old school desk. In the corner is a moth-eaten purple armchair and as he turns to face me, I notice an open briefcase on the desk and it contains ... a small, shiny hammer.

Well into his sixties, the physician presents a rather portly figure in his dark cherry waist-coat which conceals faded braces doing their utmost to support a pair of baggy navy-blue trousers. He is old, bent and bald, but he greets me with the toothy smile of a man who is about to make some serious coin.

"Narthen, lad. What's ter do, eh?"

Unprepared for such a far-reaching and detailed medical question, I managed a fairly succinct summary of my current medical plight. Choosing to echo my physician's level of technical and knowledgeable vocabulary, I indicated the general area of my complaint:

"It's me leg - it's bloody killing me dahn 'ere..."

"Oh well then, lad, we'd best be 'avin a look at it. Tek thi clooaths off dahn ter thi underpants - tha can leave 'em on yon chair-back if tha wants..." and he indicated the dowdy purple armchair in the corner.

So, after laying my clothes carefully across the back of the chair, I find myself once again clad only in Y-fronts and socks, occupying the front-room of a complete stranger, who is this time armed with a little silver hammer! Not only that, he advances towards me, a knowing glint in his eye, and bids me bend over an upright chair by the window.

Convinced that I am about to feature in some kind of pornographic film item for sale on the seamier stalls of Batley market, I hesitate. After a fleeting moment's consideration, however, I eventually comply with his instruction, such is my desire to take to the green sod again in the proud name of Wheelwright Old Boys F.C.

With a great deal of knowledgeable muttering and confirmatory mumbling, he rubs his gnarled old hand up and down my bared leg as I strain my ears for the whirr of a rolling 8mm cine-camera. But the only sound I hear is a smart tap as he gives the lumbar area of my spine a vigorous clout with his little hammer.

"Reight, lad... Get thisen dressed... Tha'll be as reight as a bobbin' nar. An' that'll be four an' a tanner, if you please. Mind t'dog on thi way aht - 'e's gerrin on a bit nar, tha sees, an' 'e weeant move ser fast - oh an' send t'next un in, will ta?"

Back out on the dingy, dirty street, I dance for joy at the thought of being totally and utterly cured. I hop-skip on the cobbled pavement outside, joyfully, rapturously, anticipating pulling on the Number Five jersey this coming September. But by the time I'd descended the steepling slope back onto Bradford Road, the shooting pain down my leg was already telling me that I'd just wasted four and a tanner.

Depressed and dismal, I made my weary way back to my classroom and hoisted a sad leg onto the front desk-top...

The season dawned and began to flourish and I remained a forlorn and dejected figure on the touchline. Sometimes bent double, sometimes clutching my knee to my chest I struggle desperately to alleviate the shooting pains down the offending limb. Standing on one leg like this, I look for all the world like a deranged flamingo, hopping up

154

and down on the touchline and shouting words of encouragement born of frustration. I travelled with the First XI, desperate to play again.

Keeping an ear close to the ground in the fervent hope of finding some "alternative" remedy for my long-standing ailment becomes quite a hobby. And by the spring of '73, I think I've found it.

Again by hearsay and word of mouth, I discover the existence of a highly trained and successful local osteopath whose practice is appropriately situated in Bonegate Road. According to my several informants, this man has a proven track record of success, so like a shot from a gun, I zip off to consult with the maestro...

One fine Wednesday evening in March finds me making my way up the little winding path of "Oak Apple Cottage", past the tastefully tended rows of hollyhocks and geraniums towards the low, quaint building in front of me. I tug on the ancient bell- pull and I'm admitted by a thin, angular gentleman with grey hair and glasses. I'm shown in to a "surgery" containing shelves of worthy medical tomes and racks of small medicinal pill-bottles.

Although this is still somebody's converted front-room, I banish the memories of my Bradford Road encounter and begin to feel far more confident of a successful outcome. This is reinforced by the sight of a long, raised couch affair which gives the room a "hospital" look.

It isn't long, however, before nagging memories of recent consultations begin to raise their ugly heads when I am instructed to take off all clothing except Y-fronts and socks. Oh no, I think - here we go again!

But this meeting has a decidedly different flavour to all the previous consultations.

After initial discussion of my problem, during which I feel acute embarrassment at my state of undress, I am invited to lie face-down on the afore-mentioned couch. My physician then approaches my side and is so close I can feel the waft of his breath across the back of my neck. With this, I am extremely uncomfortable.

My generation of Batley Grammar School lads has a built-in anathema to blokes getting physically close to other blokes, let alone breathing on them - and me with next to nothing on! A feeling of inner disgust begins to well up in my heaving chest, and it almost erupts into a frenzied yell of fear when I feel the physician's silky hands stroking the hollow of my back! However, I am determined to take the field for the Wheelwright once again, so I heroically stifle the distasteful loathing which is churning away in the pit of my stomach and I try to listen carefully to what my physician is saying.

There is a good deal of technical mumbo-jumbo and incantation in the one-sided conversation, all of which leaves me streets behind. In my face down position, I am just about to doze off, when I am instructed to stand up and turn my back. A mild wave of panic wells in my breast - I have nothing to protect me save for my Y-fronts.

The panic turns to sweaty fear when my physician turns round and links arms, so that we are in the bum-to-bum position - after the fashion of a play-ground game we used to play as kids: You bend your back and hoist your mate while he flings his legs skywards; when he touches down on the return trip, momentum and gravity do the same for you.

Now this is alright when you're nine or ten, swinging up and down to while away a play-time or two, but not when you're a respectable schoolteacher in his mid-twenties. But, believe you me, this is what my physician did to me, foregoing, however, the joy of the reciprocal pleasure trip for himself. So I get all the fun - clad only in Y-fronts and socks, legs flying into the air, swung up on the old chap's bent back perhaps six or seven times.

"Oh joy," I thought to myself as my feet crashed to the floor for the seventh time and he brought the consultation and associated activities to an abrupt end.

"Get dressed... and take one of these pills daily until they're finished," he said imperiously. "Seaweed, y'know - excellent for the treatment of your complaint. That'll be £8.50, please." [By now, decimalisation had arrived in West Yorkshire.]

There followed a series of weekly consultations in similar vein until, after six or seven weeks and a fearful lot of laundry [clean Y-fronts every visit], I decided to call it a day. I was still a touch-line spectator at First XI games. I was still bent double and suffering pain down the leg. I still taught my classes with one leg up.

Despondent and dejected, I left Oak Apple Cottage one April evening, resigned to my fate - six months off work, a steel corset, an operation, but worst tragedy of all - *no more football...*

Until twenty-stone Angus from next door informed me, in graphic detail, of his encounter with a highly qualified and experienced osteopath in Huddersfield.

"Crippled, Ah wor - aye absolutely buggered," he recalled. "Ah couldn't even get to t'Lodge for t'monthly meetings. She [nodding towards his wife] 'ed ter bring mi dinner up ter bed for me - dint yer, luv? An' when Ah gorrup, Ah 'ed ter lie on t'floor all t'bloody day long. Anyrooad, they sent me from work ter see this feller - an' dusta know - 'e put me reight. Ah trotted aht o' theer like a spring chicken. Nivver look'd back since - reight as a bobbin... Tha' wants to give 'im a ring an get thisen fixed up. 'Course, it'll cost thi, tha knows - 'e's nooan cheap..."

The words "*reight as a bobbin*" sounded immediate alarm bells, recalling memories of Bradford Road side-streets, fat smelly Labradors and little shiny hammers. I am tempted to shelve Angus's sincere, well-meant advice somewhere in the dark and dusty recesses of my mind and dream of what might have been, thereby saving myself a few precious bob.

But you know how it is when you're in pain and desperate for some relief - you'll try anything. [Besides, I'm still hankering after just one more appearance in the Wheelwright Number 5 shirt]. So a fine May evening in 1974 found me hobbling in pain along Queen Street in the shadows of Huddersfield Polytechnic. I hold yet another one-sided conversation with myself about my quest for a return to the green playing-fields of the Old Boys' League.

Was it now assuming the proportions of Chamberlain's 1939 expedition for Peace in our Time...?

My doubts were soon dispelled, however, when I reached the premises of one A.K.Burton. *"Registered Osteopath and Member of the British School of Osteopathy"*.

That's what I read on the brass plaque mounted on the Yorkshire stone wall at the foot of a set of wide impressive steps. The setting sun glints on the polished brass as I make my way inside, to be met by a *Receptionist*.

This is no Bradford Road Back Street Crank; neither is it a Bonegate Road Bum-to-Bum Bloke. This is *quality* - proper attention at last. No more prancing about in somebody's front room with 90% of your kit off, because here, in Huddersfield, you are shown to a small cubicle after your brief stay in the Waiting Room. Proper X-rays are taken and A.K.Burton himself sits down with you and discusses the results - and informs you that, without doubt, you will be playing football again in twelve months' time.

I didn't quite leave the consultation with the energy of a spring chicken but already I felt a whole lot better! Football in twelve months' time and the promise of a total cure - the prospect was almost delicious enough to eat! Of course, the treatment would be long, difficult and expensive but boy, was it going to be worth it! I returned home from school the following day a new man - without once having had to rest my leg on the front desk.

Imagine, then, my crest-fallen disappointment as I attend for my first session with A.K.Burton and am instructed by the Receptionist to go upstairs to my cubicle and strip off to Y-fronts and socks! A small bubble of enthusiasm bursts as I think to myself :"Back to semi-nudity..."

I enter the consulting room sheepishly and notice the hospital-like raised couch affair. A slightly larger bubble bursts as A.K. Burton instructs me to lie face down on it. But the biggest bubble of all bursts when the great man lays his silken hands on my back and gently strokes me up and down, passing pleasanteries about the weather and his recent reading of "Zen and the Art of Motor-Cycle Maintenance".

But I am totally unprepared for A.K.'s next medical manouevre which frightens me out of my schoolmasterly wits the first time it happened...

After far too much stroking and gentle stretching for my Shoddy Town liking, A.K. says that he is going to arrange me [my body] into a position suitable for the next phase of my treatment.

"Will this necessitate the removal of any more clothing..." I ask, "since I have very little left?"

"No, not at all," smiles A.K. and he proceeds to bend and re-shape my body by rolling me over onto my side and gathering my torso up into a position reminiscent of a foetal crouch. One leg, however, is extended straight down the bed and the other drawn up underneath as in the afore-mentioned womb-like position.

"Now just relax..." smiles A.K., and he leans over me with his mouth about three inches from my ear.

Now this is more than red-blooded Shoddy Town flesh and blood can stand, and in a state of abject terror, I prepare myself for the tender ear-nibbling and the pas-sionate kiss which I am certain is to follow. I clench a mean fist, ready to clout the sod if he so much as makes a move towards my ear-lobe, all the while promising myself that I will not tell a soul about this back in the Wheelwright dressing-room. Not one syllable shall pass these tightly sealed lips - I'll never live it down if I so much as utter a word...

By now, I've averted my head, ducking the expected pucker and slobbering embrace. But out of the blue, A.K. raises his entire upper torso *away* from my vulnerable ear-lobe and my prone and helpless contorted body, and he smashes down on me with his full weight.

The air leaves my chest cavity with a rasping sort of a grunt that could be heard in Dewsbury Bus Station. There is a loud jarring crack of bone against bone somewhere in my dorsal region and A.K. concludes the day's events with a polite "Thank you very much. See you on Thursday - good night..."

Off he goes into the next room, rubbing his hands in preparation for an assault on the next poor, unsuspecting bugger...

A.K.'s assaults about my person continued for about eight or nine weeks - twice a week - contributing significantly to my rapidly dwindling bank balance. The improvements in my dorsal area were - nil, and I was still teaching with one leg up. The occupants of the front desk were getting a bit peeved about the dirty footmarks on their GCE Coursework essays and had complained to my Head of Department.

But far more important than all that, I had begun to sense that the playing fields of the Yorkshire Old Boys' League were once again fading away on the mists of time and incapacity. So one evening, I ventured to mention the fact to A.K.

"Er...Perhaps, by now ... er ... as my treatment has been proceeding for some time... er... um, I thought that perhaps there might have been some ... er... that is ... I'd rather hoped that I'd be playing football by now..." I hesitantly mentioned, whilst his mouth was poised [but not puckered] the regulation three inches from my ear-lobe. "But I'm still experiencing a fair amount of pain down my ... er ... leg..."

"Oh yes, of course..." was A.K.'s knowledgeable reply.

"Just as I expected, but now we are ready for the next phase of your treatment. This is something a little different... something I've been working on for quite some time now..." and he rolled me over onto my back, legs straight down the bed, hands across the chest in the funereal coffin position. And while I'm left reflecting on the fact that my treatment had begun with the birth position and now here I was in the death position, A.K. creeps silently round the head of the couch, out of sight.

Huge doubts about the whole venture begin to billow up in my mind: "The man's a nutter, stroking me and smacking my puny body about, bouncing up and down on it whenever it suits him; satisfying his twisted and perverted desires while I shell out hard-earned brass for the privilege. I make the long trek back and forth from the depths of outer Batley twice weekly, and there's sod all to report".

I'm just about to get up off the couch and tell the man where to stick his Osteopathic Theories when I feel his slender silken fingers slide down either side of my neck, smoothing down the hairs on it which immediately leap erect in trouser-filling terror. As his strong, steely grip tightens down either side of my neck, a little voice whines in my head: "The bastard's going to strangle you!" and I prepare to meet my Maker...

"Now just relax...." says A.K. in his usual reassuring manner and visions of the Pearly Gates become somewhat misty as I calm down a bit. I am lulled into a false sense of security. "Let yourself go limp and.... Relax," just like a well-rehearsed hypnotist.

My trembling terror begins to ebb away as the rigid stiffness of fear gradually seeps out of my thighs. It drains into my calves and out through my toes to the soothing sound of A.K's reassuring tone.

And then comes the finale.

With an ever-tightening vice-like grip, he deftly wrenches my head and snaps it vigorously from left to right at 90 degrees to my horizontal body. I hear a rending crack in my ears - the crack of several shattering vertebrae, no doubt - and a shaft of pain sears down my spine.

My legs leap involuntarily into the air as I let out a heartfelt bellow of anguish: "You lousy bastard - you've broken my bloody neck!!!"

Leaping off the couch to confront my tormentor, I continue: "Call yourself a medical man! You've damn near ripped my soddin' head off! I can't feel a bloody thing in my throat - you've numbed it to buggery..." and I stagger around the treatment room clutching the back of my neck like Bert Trautmann in the 1956 FA Cup Final.

"What the hell am I going to do now? Look at me! I can hardly bloody walk - who's going to drive me home ?" But my words trailed and trickled away into a thick and embarrassed silence as the truth dawned ...

THE PAIN IN MY LEG HAD GONE !

For the first time in two whole years, there was no knifing ache down to where my sock would have been were I not clad only in my Y-fronts...

*

How sweet were my last eight seasons on the green fields of the Yorkshire Old Boys' League!

I captained the Wheelwright Old Boys Third XI, proudly wearing the Number 5 shirt [along with an extra-specially-wide, whale-bone reinforced JS* for back support].

In the Bermuda Triangle of my twilight years, bounded by Soldiers' Fields in Leeds, Salendine Nook in Huddersfield and Spencer Road in Bradford, I relished every

---

*JS: jock-strap, a knacker-pouch on a belt, worn by many sportsmen. I once saw Paul Shackleton[Old Batelians] play the game of his life when a dressing-room prankster liberally creamed the inside of his JS with Fiery Jack ointment. At full-time, Shack's inner thighs were the colour of pickled beetroot.

"You've damned near ripped my soddin' head off..!"

incident-filled moment of every ninety-minute session of every Saturday afternoon. It was a rapturous delight to play in a Cup Final and to receive only the second medal of my entire footballing career: Yorkshire Old Boys' League White Trophy [Third XI's] Runners-up, 1979.

But the most rewarding sentiment is one that the years have kept closely guarded and, until now, tightly locked away...

What price the Specialist who writes you off and dismisses you with a cursory flap of the hand: *"Oh, Good God, man! I very much doubt that you'll ever play again."?*

I often wonder to what girth his oak-panelled wallet expanded as he ushered away other poor, unsuspecting sufferers to get on with their wrecked lives. For without the fervent desire to run around half-naked on the football fields of West Yorkshire, perhaps I would have joined them, believing myself to be written off and finished - a decrepit has-been - because the Specialist said so.

Not for me the drooped shoulders shuffling off into senility, the carpet-slippers, walking stick and steel corset ... Oh no!

I proudly played centre-half for Wheelwright Old Boys with all the enthusiasm of a ten year old, until maturity, responsibility and threats of divorce got the better of my conscience.

Be upstanding one and all, and raise your glasses to Eternal Optimism, A.K.Burton [Registered Osteopath] and Alternative Medicine!

***

ENDPIECE

The misty fog-bound curtain of long-gone memories finally descends on those soot-blackened mill chimneys of yesterday, so it's about time to stop now. After all, when this game kicked off, nobody had even heard of Elvis Presley's footwear*, "Rock Around the Clock" was about to make Bill Haley's kiss-curl recognisable the world over, and Alf Ramsey played right back for England. As you might expect, the Shoddy Towns are but shadows of their former great selves, but when you've lived and worked here for the best part of forty-five years, the gilt-edged memories of the happy past are only a chance encounter away...

I drove past Taylor's Batley mill the other day - at the intersection of Mayman and Blakeridge Lanes. The name is still there in peeling maroon and white on the huge square tower - J.T. & J. Taylor - but it stands forlorn now, impotent and useless, utilised by Modern Times as an aerial mast for mobile phones.

In its giant shadow looms, bedraggled and dejected, the massive dark mill which once was home to the clattering hum of a hundred Washbowl Willeys and Edge-trim Pickers. Some of the windows in the great five-storey building have been boarded up; others stand open to the four winds. This mighty edifice stands silent sentinel over a deserted mill yard where weeds and cast-off tyres are the only signs of a Shoddy Town life once vibrant with the economic activity of the day: "earning an honest crust"...

Not that I'd noticed all this. I'm on my nippy adolescent way up the nostalgic stairs of the big red Number 21 Yorkshire Woollen District Transport bus [Huddersfield-Leeds via Batley] as it rounds the corner of Upper Commercial Street. I dive onto the maroon-upholstered

* Blue Suede Shoes

back seat and pay my threepence fare to the blue-uniformed conductor. After he whistles his happy way down the steps to his station on the rear platform, I snuggle down into the welcoming warmth of the top deck for a satisfying Woodbine. The journey home over Healey, through Heckmondwike and on to the Bar House at Liversedge is my yester-year haunt for the next five minutes...

Ruefully, I light up a current version of the "Great Little Cigarette" and ponder the fact that I'm still an avid user of the diabolical weeds.

Four English pounds [and more] for a packet of twenty is the current rate of exchange, and I agonise yet again over the fact that I used to buy one Woodie and two matches for threepence on the way home from school. And what's more, they're probably killing me. Not that Death is a stranger in my life anymore.

My Mum and Dad, both of whom were responsible for my coming to the Heavy Woollen District in the first place, are long gone. And only the other day, I heard that both of the A-form RAF Brylcreem Boys from that first Duke of Edinburgh's Award sortie had passed on to the Great Expedition in the Sky.

'Now perhaps, if they'd shared their bacon rashers that fine Dales morning all those years ago, things might have turned out differently...,' I muse, lost in a rêverie of wild horses and dried egg.

As my old blue estate car rolls slowly to a halt at the "new" traffic-lights, I pass an internal memo to myself: The time is now to change this vehicle which I have come to know and love over the past four years. This will mean a visit to H. Mitchell Car Sales of Staincliffe, my car-dealer for a number of Shoddy Town years now.

I recall fondly that my last three cars have all been purchased from *the* leading second-hand car dealer in the Heavy Woollen District - "Vehicles to suit all tastes & budgets - Family run business". The owner is an ex-Rugby League professional, craggy now in his old-age but still with the glint of yester-year fun in those steel-grey eyes. That fifty-six year old meaty fist of his once fastened round my throat up the snicket on the top cinder-track at Batley Grammar School. It was he who instructed me to "say summat" for the general entertainment and delight of the assembled crowd, and can thus be held responsible for my 45 year old Shoddy Town accent. But nowadays, Haydn Mitchell [Form Bully, no less] is a life-long friend, yesterday's threats have long been forgotten, and "Mitch" is the finest car-dealer west of the M1.

Perhaps his opportunist business acumen was spawned in the library that break-time in 1957 when he hadn't done his Maths homework and we were due for a test on it during the next lesson. Failure to achieve at least $^7/_{10}$ meant an automatic Saturday morning detention from Charlie Spurr, so Mitch just *had* to avoid taking that test.

The resulting ploy was the sharpest bit of evasion it has ever been my privilege to witness. We marvelled at his brazen ingenuity and we envied him his complete success, but just how Our Hero managed to avoid the purgatory of a Saturday morning detention will have to be the subject of a future Shoddy Town Tale...

***

SHODDY TOWN SPEAK

The language of the Shoddy Towns is a weird and wonderful mode of communication. It continues to enrich our daily lives with its warmth and diversity, but it is often a mystery to the occasional visitor who might just be passing through. To a 1950's youngster from the heart of Cider-With-Rosie country, it was a foreign tongue which - embarrassingly when you're "nobbut a lad" - had to be regularly translated for comprehension purposes. The language contains its own grammatical constructions and nuances which have never featured in any learned text. Over the years, however, I have become accustomed to the niceties of its usage and thus can pass, in any neck of the woods, for a dyed in the blood, born and bred Shoddy Town lad.

This glossary contains a selection of words from my tales which may serve to enlighten a reader from beyond the Heavy Woollen District.

Glossary

bacca brass	money to be spent on cigarettes. This expression is a close relative of "jock brass": money to be spent on lunch-time repast
bahna	with the intention of; literally "going to". Interchangeable in Shoddy Town speak with "off ter", as in "Ahm off ter gie 'im a reight good 'iding" or " 'E's off ter t'fish-oil fer 'is tea terneet."
baht	lacking a vital article/item, as in " 'Eez come baht 'is coit"
berree	Translated as "wager against", this phrase is possibly best understood by reference to the well known Shoddy Town expression:

"Eesezeeazburrahberreeant". A literal translation would be: "he avows that he has, but I'll wager that he has not."

broddle	to poke about vigorously with an implement, usually inserted into some narrow cavity
capped	surprised and amazed, as in "By, Ah wor fair capped..."
catch thi deeath	suffer from exposure. A well-known phrase from the National Anthem of Yorkshire "On Ilkley Moor Baht 'at."
cobbin'	passing articles out of the alimentary canal via the rectum. Often used in the context of abject fear
coit	overcoat
copped	caught out doing something illegal
dadn't	a curious negative expression meaning "dare not", it has no positive counterpart. i.e. no self-respecting Shoddy Town resident will ever be heard to utter " 'e dad do it...."
dusta	literally, "do you" as in "Dusta think so?" or "Dusta wanna cupper tea?"
gie it some pasty	approach the task in hand with energy, verve and gusto. Often interchangeable with "gie it some welly."
gip	to wretch as if about to be sick, but not quite getting there

laik/laikin'	of children and sportsmen, play/ playing. When used of other adults, it means not at one's place of employ during the course of a normal working day.
maun't	might not/must not, often delivered as a salutory warning: "tha maun't miss t'bus else tha'll be late for thi work..."
mawks	hands; in particular, curious, interfering types
mesen	for grammatical purists, the first person refelexive pronoun. For students of a foreign language at Batley Grammar School in the 50's, such pronouns had to be conjugated thus:

Singular	Plural
missen	ussens
thissen	thissens
issen, erssen	theirsens

neb	the peak of a cap
nobbut	only; insignificant. " 'E's nobbut a lad" meaning "he is but young and thus unimportant"
nooan	the negative "not". eg " 'Ee's nooan 'avin' none on it. Ah'm keepin' it for mesen"
offter	see "bahna"
oil	literally "hole" but in usage, it can mean "place". [see "piss-oil] During my first week at Batley Grammar School, I was the butt of much derisory laughter when I expressed bafflement at the

phrase: "Oh, thee - put t'wood in t'oil, will ta?" I discovered later that this was a polite request to close the door.

pillock — a useless, silly person

piss-oil — toilet, using "oil" to mean "place" Thus, "cellar-oil" - a place below stairs; "cardin'-oil" - a place where wool is processed

reight as a bobbin — on a spinning machine, a bobbin was a spool for winding on wool. Presumably, if any bobbin in a row on the machine was out of line or incorrectly installed, the effects would be drastic, particularly on the wage of the machine-minder. Hence, all your "bobbins" have to be "reight" [right] for success to be achieved.

sarnies — sandwiches

Sat'day — at Batley Grammar School, a two hour detention on a Saturday morning - an excellent deterrent to *any* kind of academic failure

snap — light lunch-time repast, often carried in a small tin; interchange able with "jock"

snicket — a narrow pathway between two walls or hedges. Opinions vary as to its relationship with that other narrow pathway, known as a ginnel. In either case, they provided handy escape routes and/or hiding places when you were pursued and/or in need of a sly swaller.

tab-end	the very last vestiges of a smoked cigarette
tacklin'	the male genitalia. Sometimes referred to as "weddin' tacklin'"
tanner	for those born before 1970, sixpence [when there were twelve pennies in a shilling]. Along with bobs, half-dollars and other gigantic monetary pieces, it guaranteed the sag to the knees of many regulation grey, long-short trousers in the '50s.
wazzock	derogatory noun of undetermined meaning; Obviously a term of abuse, any user of it was safe from recrimination since no dictionary definition exists
weean't	will not be successful in an attempt to do something
terneet	tonight
yond	that one over there
up to press	up to, and including, this moment in time

***

Lightning Source UK Ltd.
Milton Keynes UK
23 September 2010

160260UK00001BA/13/A